# Fifth Grade Science

*For Home School or Extra Practice*

**By Thomas Bell**

**Home School Brew Press**

**www.HomeSchoolBrew.com**

**Cover Image © Mat Hayward - Fotolia.com**

**Table of Contents**

**Disclaimer**

*This book was developed for parents and students of no particular state; while it is based on common core standards, it is always best to check with your state board to see what will be included on testing.*

# About Us

Homeschool Brew was started for one simple reason: to make affordable Homeschooling books! When we began looking into homeschooling our own children, we were astonished at the cost of curriculum. Nobody ever said homeschool was easy, but we didn't know that the cost to get materials would leave us broke.

We began partnering with educators and parents to start producing the same kind of quality content that you expect in expensive books...but at a price anyone can afford.

We are still in our infancy stages, but we will be adding more books every month. We value your feedback, so if you have any comments about what you like or how we can do better, then please let us know!

To add your name to our mailing list, go here: http://www.homeschoolbrew.com/mailing-list.html

# Chapter 1: Scientific Investigation

Science is the study of both living and non-living things. It involves studying both the physical and natural world through the use of observation and experiments. It is the job of a scientist to investigate the world.

Scientific investigation is an amazing thing that allows knowledge to grow and advance. That is because today's advancements are all built on what other scientists have learned before. The key to any these scientific investigations, past or present, is evidence. **Evidence** is what all scientists must use to show or confirm that the statements about their investigations are true: and the more plentiful the evidence, the more valid the investigation. That's because we cannot rely on someone just simply saying, "The Earth is round!" We need evidence, and loads of it, to verify it is true.

But since we live in such an enormous and complex world, exactly how do scientists approach getting evidence and in turn finding answers to how the world works?

The process that scientists use to study, learn, and investigate scientific questions is called the **Scientific Method**. It can be used for any branch of science and by scientists of any age, even by young scientists like you. Whatever scientists wish to study, from the spots on a leaf to the stars in the universe, the steps of the Scientific Method allow them to do so and learn in a logical, organized way. The basic steps of the Scientific Method are:

**1. Question**

**2. Research**

**3. Hypothesis**

**4. Procedure/Method**

**5. Data**

**6. Observations**

**7. Conclusion**

**8. New Question**

What does that have to do with you? Well, as a young, new scientist, it is your job to take your knowledge about science and the world around you and use it in your own **experiments** and **observations**. So how do you get started?

To begin, all a scientist needs to do is ask a **question**. After observing the world, something perks the interest and curiosity from which a question can be asked. The trick is that the question must be something that can be measured. The question usually begins with what, why, how, where or when.

List three questions you have about the world around you. The best questions come from observations you have made and that could be used to help you conduct an experiment.

1. Why isn't the water clear in the ocean?

2. Why do they name Tropical storms?? 😊

3. Why can't koulas live in America

Now, to get focused and organized, the next step is to gather some basic information about the topic in question. Doing some basic **research** will help greatly with the next step.

So, let's say you wondered if a plant can grow in the dark. With a little research, you find that different plants need different amounts of sunlight, but light is necessary for the plant to grow. So, the **question** might be, "What happens to a plant that gets no sunlight?"

It is now time to create a **hypothesis**. A hypothesis is a fancy word for an educated guess. Your hypothesis is simply a brief statement (one sentence) about what you think the answer is to the question. The hypothesis could then be, "Plants grown best in sunlight not in the dark." After a hypothesis has been proposed, the experimental part of the process can begin which will prove the hypothesis correct or incorrect. Don't worry about whether a hypothesis is right or wrong. You can learn just as much about the topic with an incorrect hypothesis.

Designing the steps of the experiment is next. This is called the **procedure,** or sometimes the method. Here, a step-by-step plan or guide is designed which serve as directions. The materials needed are also included. It's a lot like a recipe only the outcome is not to bake a cake, but to explore a scientific question. The procedure further allows a scientist to organize their ideas and helps avoid some problems that could possibly occur during the experiment.

When writing the procedures or designing an experiment, it is important to test or manipulate only *one* **variable** at a time. An experiment is based on cause and effect. That means changing one item causes something else to change in a predictable way. A **variable** is a changing quantity in the cause and effect of the experiment. For example, if we want to design an experiment to find out if plants grow in the dark, we only want to change *one* thing (one variable), the amount of light a plant gets. We do not want to change other variables like the type of plant, the amount of water, or type of soil. If we keep the other variables the same, we can most accurately measure and observe what happens to a plant that gets no light.

And now…finally… the experiment can begin. The next step takes place during the experiment: collecting **data**. Data is information collected through trials and tests. The data can often be **numerical** or use numbers that measure something, such as height, length, time, rate, etc. Displaying the data in a visual way like with a **graphs** or **charts** is an effective way to provide evidence. Data can also be in the form of sketches or photos. Collecting data is not the only tool that allows scientists to prove their hypothesis, however.

**Observations** is the next step of the Scientific Method. It is written descriptions of what was noticed during the experiment beyond the numerical data. Record things you notice like color, texture, smell, as well as errors, uncontrolled variables and anything surprising or unexpected. Also include in your observations anything you noticed from sketches or photos.

It is now time for the last step, the **conclusion**. After carefully recording the data and observations, the information now can be examined and analyzed. Basically, a scientist uses their ability of analysis to answer the original question. The conclusion, then, is a brief statement that tells if the results of the experiment either support or oppose the hypothesis. Sometimes, however, the results are inconclusive. That means there was not enough data or observations that can be used as evidence to support or negate the hypothesis. Whether the conclusion supports or opposes the hypothesis, or the results are inconclusive, the experiment is still valid and a new question can usually be formulated, and the process can start again. And, that's the beauty of scientific investigation! It is a continuing process that builds on what was learned before.

You can review the steps of the Scientific Method in the chart below:

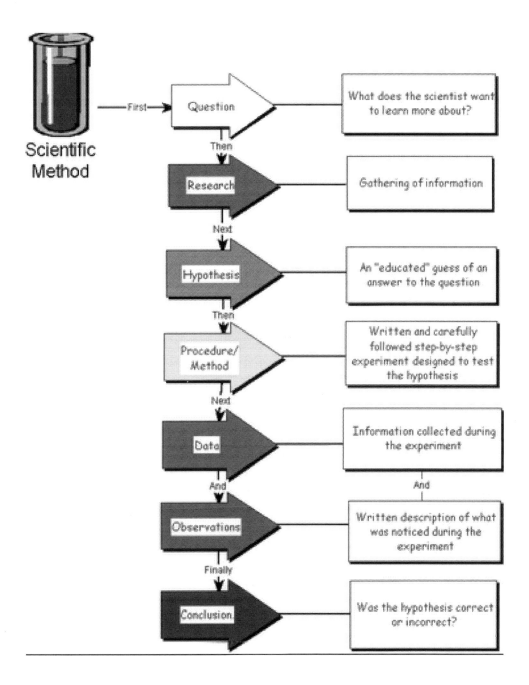

Scientific
Method

First → Question

What does the scientist want
to learn more about?

Then

Research

Gathering of information

Next

Hypothesis

An "educated" guess of an
answer to the question

Then

Procedure/
Method

Written and carefully
followed step-by-step
experiment designed to test
the hypothesis

Next

Data

Information collected during
the experiment

And

And

Observations

Written description of what
was noticed during the
experiment

Finally

Conclusion

Was the hypothesis correct
or incorrect?

# Experiments in the Scientific Method

You've learned the steps of the Scientific Method and how the process of designing experiments and collecting evidence or data allows you to come to conclusions about questions you have. Now, let's put what you've learned into practice with experiments that help you better understand and tackle the steps of the Scientific Method.

**1. Question: How can you tell if an egg is raw or hardboiled?**

**Research:** Think about what you already know about the structure of raw eggs vs. hardboiled eggs. Find out how a raw egg is different than a hardboiled egg and how liquids act when spun inside a container.

**Materials**: 1 raw egg and 1 hardboiled egg (Note: the hard boiled egg needs to be refrigerated long enough to be the same temperature as the raw egg); a paper and pencil; permanent marker

**Hypothesis**: Write your own educated guess as a statement that answers the question.

**Procedure**:
o Label each egg raw or hardboiled with the permanent marker. Label your paper with two columns: "raw" and "hardboiled" and the numbers 1, 2, and 3 underneath each word.

o Gently spin the raw egg on a large, flat surface. Touch the egg gently while spinning.

o Record your observations about the movement of the egg while spinning. Repeat for a total of 3 trials.

o Repeat steps 2 and 3 for the hardboiled egg.

**Data:** Analyze your observations while the eggs were spinning.

**Observations:** The raw egg should wobble while spinning. The hardboiled egg should stop spinning as soon as it's touch.

**Conclusion:** Because the raw egg has a liquid center, it keeps spinning due to inertia (a body in motion, stays in motion). When you stop it, only the shell stops and the liquid inside keeps spinning. The raw egg is solid, so when stopped, the whole thing stops.

**New Question:** Write questions about any new ideas or wonderings that this experiment brings to mind.

**2. Question: Do all liquids weigh the same?** (If we pour liquids into a column (without shaking), will they mix together or will they stay in their own position in layers?)

**Research:** Think about what you already know about different types of liquids layer and interact when put together.

**Materials**:

- ¼ cup (60 ml) baby oil
- ¼ cup (60 ml) rubbing alcohol
- ¼ cup (60 ml) vegetable oil (yellow)
- ¼ cup (60 ml) water
- ¼ cup (60 ml) dishwashing liquid (blue)
- ¼ cup light Karo corn syrup
- ¼ cup (60 ml) honey
- one 12 ounce (350ml) glass or clear plastic cup
- food coloring
- several (2-5) other cups for mixing

**Hypothesis**: Write your own educated guess as a statement that answers the question. List the liquids in the order that you predict they will layer or if they will mix.

**Procedure**:

o In separate cups, mix a few drops of food coloring into each of the liquids. Make the baby oil red, the rubbing alcohol orange (mix red and yellow), the water green (mix blue and yellow), and the Karo syrup purple (mix red and blue).

o Start by pouring the honey into the clear container. Be careful to pour the honey directly into the center; avoid the honey dripping down the sides.
o Pour each liquid SLOWLY into the container, one at a time, in the order listed below. Make sure to pour the liquids slowly and into the center of the cylinder so that the liquids do not touch the sides of the container. (*The liquids will mix a little while pouring.*)

Pour the liquids into the container in the following order:

- Honey
- Karo syrup
- Dish soap
- Water
- Vegetable oil
- Rubbing alcohol
- baby oil

o Observe as the liquid layers even themselves out because of the varying densities.

**Data:** Record how the liquids layered.

**Observations:** The liquids should layer in the following order:

| |
|---|
| baby oil |
| rubbing alcohol |
| yellow vegetable oil |
| water |
| blue dishwashing liquid |
| light Karo syrup (corn syrup) |
| honey |

**Conclusion:** Each liquid has its own density. All liquid densities are measured in comparison to water. Water has a density of 1.00. If a liquid has a density greater than water, the liquid's density has a value greater than 1. If the liquid has a density less than water, the liquid has a density less than 1.00. The following table shows densities of liquid compared to water:

| | |
|---|---|
| baby oil | .82 |
| rubbing alcohol | .87 |

| | |
|---|---|
| yellow vegetable oil | .91 |
| water | 1.00 |
| blue dishwashing liquid | 1.03 |
| light Karo syrup (corn syrup) | 1.33 |
| honey | 1.36 |

**New Question:** Write questions about any new ideas or wonderings that this experiment brings to mind.

## 3. Question: Where is the safest place to store bread so that mold won't grow?

**Research:** Think about what you already know about how and where mold grows on bread. Find out where mold grows best.

**Materials**: 6 slices of bread; plastic baggies; a teaspoon; a paper and pencil; permanent marker

**Hypothesis**: Write your own educated guess as a statement that answers the question.

**Procedure**:

o Label six (6) plastic sandwich-size bags with the following conditions and current date:

- •#1 dry/warm/light
- •#2 moist/warm/light
- •#3 dry/warm/dark
- •#4 moist/warm/dark
- •#5 dry/cool
- •#6 moist/cool

o Place one (1) slice of bread into each plastic bag marked "dry", avoiding contact with any water.

o Sprinkle three (3) slices of bread with 2 teaspoon of water. Place in the bags labeled with the word moist (#2, #4 and #6).

o Seal all six (6) plastic bags. Make sure each is thoroughly closed.

o Place the bags with a slice of bread inside in the following locations:

| On the kitchen counter (where it gets at least **5 hours of natural sunlight**): | In a closed, dark kitchen cupboard: | In the refrigerator: |
|---|---|---|
| #1 dry/warm/light | #3 dry/warm/dark | #5 dry/cool |
| #2 moist/warm/light | #4 moist/warm/dark | #6 moist/cool |

o Avoid touching, smelling or eating any of the baggies of bread.

o Each day, for seven (7) days, record any mold growth using sketches and/or photos and words.

**Data:** Describe the size and color of the mold colonies each day.

**Observations:** Baggie #4 (moist/warm/dark) should have the most mold spores, while baggie #5 (dry/cool) should have the least mold spores.

**Conclusion:** Was your hypothesis correct? Mold grows best where it is dark, warm (room temperature) and moist. To best avoid mold spores finding a host (like bread), bread should be stored in a dry, cool place like the refrigerator.

**New Question:** Write questions about any new ideas or wonderings that this experiment brings to mind.

**4. What makes things sink or float?**

**Research:** Think about what you already know about what type of things sink and what type of things float. Find out what causes things to float.

**Materials**: a large container to hold water (like a sink or a bathtub); water; 5-10 common household items of varying weights and materials (paper clips, pencils, pens, plastic or Styrofoam cups; foil; a nail, a wooden block, a coin, a cork, etc.); paper and pencil

**Hypothesis**: Write your own educated guess as a statement that answers the question.

**Procedure**:

o List all the items you collected on the paper and predict if each will **sink** or **float**.

o Fill whatever container you are using with about 6 inches of water.

o Take one object at a time and place it gently on the surface of the water.

**Data:** Record each object as "sink" or "float" next to your prediction. Do not change your prediction if it was incorrect.

**Observations:** Though some items are heavier (like a wood block) they will sink, while lighter objects (like a paperclips) will float.

**Conclusion:** Was your hypothesis correct? Whether an object sinks or floats depends on *density* (how close together the molecules are), not weight. Any objects that were less dense than water floated! Any objects more dense than the water sank.

**New Question:** Write questions about any new ideas or wonderings that this experiment brings to mind.


**5. Does hot or cold water freeze fastest?**

**Research:** Think about what you already know about how fast a liquid freezes. Find out at what temperature water freezes.

**Materials**: a freezer; 3 plastic bowls of equal size and shape (glass bowls can crack); 2 pots to heat water; sticky labels or masking tape; a marker; water; 1 measuring cup; a thermometer; a timer; paper and pencil

**Hypothesis**: Write your own educated guess as a statement that answers the question.

**Procedure**:

o Label the three bowls cold, warm and hot.

o Clear enough space in the freezer so that you can put all three bowls in at the same time.

o Measure 1 of cup water into each of the 2 pots. With an adult's help, heat one to 70 degrees and one to 100 degrees.

o Measure 1 cup of cold tap water that is 40 degrees.

o Pour the hot (100 degrees), warm (70 degrees) and cold (40 degrees) water into corresponding pre-labeled bowls.

o Immediately place all three bowls into the freezer.

o Every 10 minutes, check the temperature of each bowl by leaving the thermometer in the water for about 15 seconds. Record the temperatures of each bowl.

o Repeat previous step until all bowls have frozen.

**Data:** Record the temperature of each bowl every ten minutes and the time at which each bowl froze.

**Observations:** The warm and/or hot water will freeze faster.

**Conclusion:** Was your hypothesis correct? Due to evaporation of the hotter water, there is less water in the bowl left to freeze. In addition, convection causes the hotter water to cool more quickly. This is called the Mpemba effect.

**New Question:** Write questions about any new ideas or wonderings that this experiment brings to mind.

# Chapter 1 Quiz

## I. Use each of the following vocabulary words to make each statement correct:

| variable | experiments | evidence | numerical | Scientific Method |
|----------|-------------|----------|-----------|-------------------|

1. _____

_ is what all scientists must use to show or confirm the statements about their investigations are true.

2. _Numerical_ data is the use numbers that measure something, such as height, length, time, rate, etc.

3. A changing quantity in the cause and effect of the experiment is called a _variable_ and only one at a time should be changed in an experiment.

4. The process that scientists use to study, learn and investigate scientific questions is called the _Scientific Method_.

5. Scientists conduct _experiments_ to find out answers to questions.

## II. Draw a line between each step of the scientific method and its definition.

6. **Question**          _Conclusion_ A statement telling whether or not the

                          hypothesis was correct

7. **Research**          _Data_ Information collected during an experiment

8. **Hypothesis**        Written description of what was noticed during

_Procedure_
_data_

an experiment

*Hypothesis* (handwritten)

**9. Procedure**

8. *Hypothesis* (handwritten)

An educated guess that answers the question

*Question* (handwritten)

**10. Data**

The topic or idea the scientist

wants to learn about

*Procedure* (handwritten)

**11. Observations**

Step-by-step directions for an experiment

*Research* (handwritten)

**12. Conclusion**

Gathering of information

**III. True or False: Answer each of the following questions by writing a T for true or F for false.**

13. Only adult biologists are considered scientists. ____

14. A hypothesis must be correct for an experiment to be valid.____

15. Science is a continuing process that builds on what was learned before. ____

16. Observations are keeping records of things that are noticed during an experiment like color, texture, smell, as well as errors, uncontrolled variables and anything surprising or unexpected ____

17. When writing the procedures or designing an experiment, it is important to test or

manipulate multiple variables at a time. _____


18. In the Scientific Method the question must be something that can be measured. _____


19. The procedure is a step-by-step plan or guide is designed which serve as directions which must also list the materials needed. _____


20. Doing some basic research will help you write a better hypothesis. _____

# Chapter 2: Changes in Matter

## What is Matter?

Matter is the "stuff" of which everything is made. Matter is anything that has mass and takes up space. All matter is made of at least one atom. The way in which matter takes up space varies in different ways. The states of matter you are most familiar with are **solids, liquids,** and **gas**. Each state is also called a **phase**. Each phase is distinct period in a process of change, that is evidence that matter **changes**.

Each **state of matter** has unique qualities:

- **Solid**-hard and holds its shape
- **Liquid**-becomes the shape of the container its in
- **Gas**-fills its container and spreads out equally

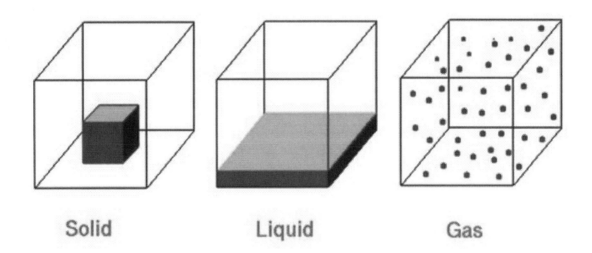

Solid          Liquid          Gas

Can you name three solids, three liquids and three gases?

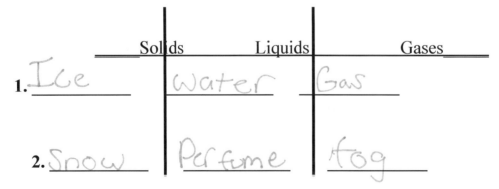

| Solids | Liquids | Gases |
|---|---|---|
| 1. Ice | Water | Gas |
| 2. Snow | Perfume | Fog |

3. Sleet      Rain      Steam

Matter can **change** in two different ways. It can go a through a **physical change** or a **chemical change**. It is very important to understand the difference.

## Physical Change vs. Chemical Change

When an element or compound goes through a **physical change,** it changes between a **solid, liquid** and **gas,** but is still the <u>same</u> thing, the same **substance**. The substance only changes form. This occurs when **energy** is either added (like an increase in temperature) or taken away (like a decrease in temperature). For example, when liquid water ($H_2O$) goes through a physical change by taking away energy (decreasing the temperature) the water changes to a solid also known as ice. And when energy is added to liquid water (increasing the temperature), the water changes to a gas that we call steam. However, even though the water ($H_2O$) changes from solid to liquid and liquid to gas, it was still always water ($H_2O$) because the molecules have not changed.

When energy is added by an increase in temperature, the molecules of water ($H_2O$) become active and begin to move around more quickly. If you give water molecules (liquid $H_2O$) enough energy, they escape their liquid phase and become a gas. Scientists called this a movement to a **higher energy state**. Physical changes, therefore, are about **energy** and **states of matter**.

Adding pressure can also make a substance go through a physical change. For example, when propane gas is pumped into a pressurized tank, it becomes liquid.

Though no new substance is created with a physical change, though the matter may change in size, shape or color. A physical change also occurs when substances mix but do not react chemically, like mixing water and sand. One way to tell if a physical change has occurred is to know that the change is reversible. Here are 7 examples of physical changes. After each one, tell how the change is reversible:

1. water freezing: _Increase temp_

2. breaking glass: _Increase temp_

3. molding clay: _Increase temp_

4. crushing a can: _?_

5. melting candle wax: _decrease Temp_

6. dissolving salt in water: _increase temperature_

7. mixing yellow marbles and green marbles: _re separating_

Now you list 3 more physical changes:

1. _Cutting hair_

2. _making slime with borax_

3. making Ice cream

Here are other physical changes that are not as easily reversible or irreversible:

- shredding paper
- cutting wood
- dehydrating fruit
- formation of crystals
- mowing grass

How then is a physical change different from a chemical change? Well, a **chemical change** is when a substance **reacts** with another substance and an entirely <u>new</u> thing is created. This happens on a much smaller level then a physical change. The molecules are actually changing and rearranging. That means a chemical change happens on a **molecular level**. The same number of atoms is involved, but the atoms rearrange themselves, resulting in a new substance. For example, when water falls on iron, the oxygen in the water reacts with the iron, and a new substance called iron oxide is formed. this is also known as rust.

Here are 7 other examples of a chemical change:

1. a log rotting

2. digesting food

3. burning wood

4. baking a cake

5. jewelry tarnishing

6. bread becoming toast

7. milk going sour

There are some signs to look for to know if a chemical change is occurring:

- gas bubbles (antacid dropped in water)
- color change (an apple turning brown)
- temperature change (burning wood)
- light is created (fireworks)
- change of smell or taste (rotting food)

Now, you list 3 more chemical changes:

1. _Coke & mentos_

2. _Kombucha_

3. _Candle burning_

# Experiments in Changes of Matter

You've learned the difference between the types of changes of matter. Now you can try some experiments that deal physical changes as well as some that deal with chemical changes.

**1. Can you break apart colors? Chromatography**

**Research:** Think about what you already know about how colors separate. Briefly find out about chromatography.

**Hypothesis:** Write your own educated guess as a statement that answers the question.

**Materials:** a coffee filter; green, orange and purple washable markers; a cup

**Procedure:**

o Lay the coffee filter flat so it lays in a circle.

o Color circles about 1 inch wide each on the coffee filter: one green, one orange and one purple.

o Wet the paper until the circles begin to "leak" or run. Set the coffee filter on a paper towel.

**Observations:**

o Record what is happening to each colored circled.

**Conclusion:**

o Is a physical or chemical change occurring?

o How do you know? What evidence supports your conclusion?

**2. Can you inflate a balloon without blowing into it?**

**Research:** Think about what you already know (or briefly research) about substances that create bubble and release gas when combined.

**Hypothesis:** Write your own educated guess as a statement that answers the question.

**Materials:** three (3) tablespoons white vinegar; two (2) teaspoons baking soda ; a jar or small bottle (one with a narrow mouth works best); a rubber band; a balloon

**Procedure:**

o Measure then pour the vinegar into the jar or bottle.

o Measure then pour the baking soda into the balloon.

o Without letting any of the baking soda spill into the jar, wrap the opening of the balloon around the mouth of the jar and attach with the rubber band.

o Pour the baking soda in the jar and let go of the balloon.

**Observations:**

o Record what happens when then baking soda mixes with the vinegar.

**Conclusion:**

o Is a physical or chemical change occurring?

o How do you know? What evidence supports your conclusion?


**3. Does steel wool rust?**

**Research:** Think about what you already know about steel and how rust forms.

**Hypothesis:** Write your own educated guess as a statement that answers the question.

**Materials:** steel wool; white vinegar; a clear container; one piece of construction paper; a thermometer

**Procedure:**

o Place a piece of steel wool in the container and pour some vinegar on the steel wool until saturated. Let soak for about one minute.

o Remove the steel wool and drain the remaining vinegar from the container.

o Cover the container with the paper and insert the thermometer by cutting a hole the width of the thermometer in the lid. Insert thermometer into the hole and record initial temperature.

o Record temperature again after 5 minutes.

**Observations:**

o Record what you see happening to the steel wool after you cover it.

**Conclusion:**

o Is a physical or chemical change occurring?

o How do you know? What evidence supports your conclusion?

## 4. Can you separate salt dissolved into water?

**Research:** Think about what you already know salt water.

**Hypothesis:** Write your own educated guess as a statement that answers the question.

**Materials:** one cup hot water; 2 tablespoons table salt; a cup; a flat ceramic plate

**Procedure:**

o Measure then pour the table salt into the water and stir until salt is dissolved.

o Pour the solution as a thin layer onto the plate.

o Set the plate in a sunny location and allow it to remain untouched for several days. Check the plate twice a day.

**Observations:**

o Record what you see happening on the plate each time you check it.

**Conclusion:**

o Is a physical or chemical change occurring?

o How do you know? What evidence supports your conclusion?

## 5. What are the properties of a polymer?

**Research:** Briefly research properties of a polymer. Think about what you already know about the properties of putty-like material such as "Slime", "Gak" or "Flubber".

**Hypothesis:** Write your own educated guess as a statement that answers the question.

**Materials:** 8oz bottle of Elmer's glue; 1 tsp. Borax; ½ cup warm water; food coloring (color of your choice); gallon size plastic baggie; mixing bowl; measuring cup; spoon

**Procedure:**

o Empty the bottle of glue into the mixing bowl, then fill the empty bottle with warm water (put the lid back on) and shake.

o Pour the glue-water mixture into the mixing bowl and mix well. Add a few drops of food coloring.

o Measure 1/2 cup of warm water and add 1 tsp. Borax. Stir.

o While stirring the glue and water mixture, slowly add the Borax and warm water. The mixture will immediately begin to turn to a polymer. Continue to mix thoroughly with your hands. Play around with your new polymer to see first hand its properties.

**Observations:**

o Record what you saw happening when the glue was mixed with the Borax and record how the polymer felt and moved (its properties).

**Conclusion:**

o Is a physical or chemical change occurring?

o How do you know? What evidence supports your conclusion?

# Chapter 2 Quiz

**I. Determine if each is a physical or chemical change. Circle the word chemical or physical.**

1. **folding paper**: chemical   physical

2. **breaking a pencil**: chemical   physical

3. **bread molding**: chemical   physical

4. **popcorn kernels popping**: chemical   physical

5. **hydrogen peroxide bubbling on a cut:** chemical   physical

6. **whipping an egg:** chemical   physical

7. **water boiling:** chemical   physical

8. **sanding wood:** chemical   physical

9. **painting a car:** chemical   physical

10. **gas igniting:** chemical  physical

**II. Answer each question below with one word or short phrase.**

11. What is the "stuff" that all things are made up of, has mass, and takes up space?

12. What type of change happens at the molecular level?

13. Which type of change is usually reversible?

14. Would a physical or chemical change produce a new odor or bubbles?

15. In what phase of matter does a substance take on the shape of the container it is in?

16. When energy is added (increasing the temperature) to a substance such as water, what is the result?

17. In a physical or chemical change do the atoms rearrange to create a new substance?

18. What is another word for a state of matter?


**III. Think like a scientist. Answer each question in 1-2 complete sentences.**

19. How could you tell if physical reaction was taking place?

20. What kind of things might occur to tell you a chemical change was occurring and a new substance was being formed?

# Chapter 3: Electricity in Matter

## The 4<sup>th</sup> State of Matter

Electricity is not matter: it is energy. **Energy** is the flow of electrons through solids, liquids and gases. Electricity consists of electrons and protons which both carry a charge. Electrons carry a **negative charge.** Protons carry **positive charge**.

There are many materials (types of matter) that allow charges to flow or move easily. These materials are called **conductors**. We say that a material **conducts electricity** if charges move easily through it. A few materials that conduct electricity are metals like silver, gold and copper, as well as carbon and salt water.

Can you think of two more conductors? _____, _____

If materials do not conduct electricity we call them **insulators**. Some common insulators are non-metals such as rubber, plastics, and glass.
Can you think of two more insulators? _____, _____

So, electricity is not matter, it moves through matter. Some matter allows charges or electricity to move through it more freely than others.

When a massive amount of energy is added to matter, it becomes electrically charged, and another type of matter is created. Yes, another type of matter exists other than solids, liquids and gases. It is called **plasma,** the **4<sup>th</sup> state of matter**. This type of matter is not very common on Earth, but it is the most common state of matter in the universe. In fact, 99% of the universe is made of plasma. That is because matter in the state of plasma requires a very special environment to continue. So, what then is plasma?
What are you thinking plasma is?_____

Plasma is the next state of matter after gas. Remember, for matter to move to a higher energy state, the atoms become more active by the addition of **heat**. In this **phase**, the atoms are **ionized**. That means sufficient energy is provided to free electrons from atoms or molecules, and both ions and electrons now exist together. So, plasma is gas that has been energized to the point that some of the electrons break free from their nucleus, but is still traveling within the nucleus. Plasma does not have a neutral charge like the other states of matter (solid, liquid and gas): plasma is both **positively charged (+)** and **negatively charged (-)** when ionized. The amount of energy required for a gas to become ionized is enormous. It is not surprising that the amount of energy required to ionize a gas also produces heat and light.

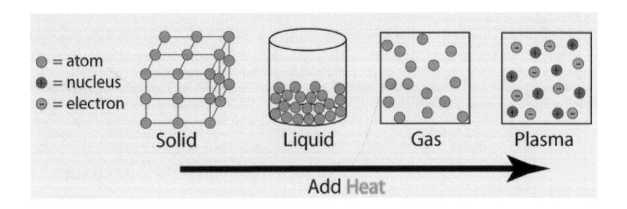

Plasmas are similar to gases. Like gases, plasmas have no definite shape and the atoms spread out equally. However, plasmas have unique properties. Plasmas particles are **electrically charged** and consist only of ions and electrons. Therefore, plasma matter carries electric currents so they conduct electricity and generate a magnetic field. Gases cannot conduct electricity, as they do not have both positive and negative charges. The image of a plasma lamp below shows the complex way that plasma behaves.

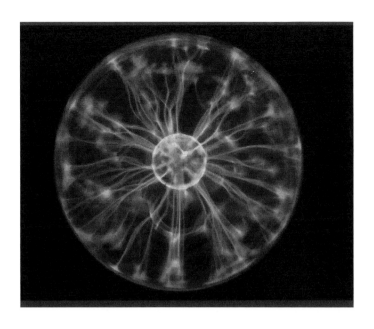

## Finding Plasmas

The most common and abundant place that plasma exists are the **stars**. Our closest neighbor, the sun, is one enormous ball of plasma. As it requires a great deal of energy to keep plasma going, it is not commonly found on Earth in nature. Plasma does exist naturally on our planet in the form of **lightning** and in the Aurora Borealis also know as **The Northern Lights**. Some plasma does not produce very high temperatures like in lightning and the stars. Man-made plasmas exists at much lower temperatures in the form of **neon signs, florescent lights** and plasma T.V.'s. Stainless steel kitchen appliances and Teflon pots and pans are also created using a plasma torch.

Solar winds made of streams of plasma are constantly being emitted from the sun. On both of the poles of the Earth, the Arctic and the Antarctic, solar winds cause an **aurora,** a natural light display. The most famous and most visible of these are at the North Pole called the **Northern Lights** or Aurora Borealis. They are also visible in the Southern Hemisphere where they are called the Aurora Australis. The Earth acts like a giant magnet and redirects or attracts electrically charged particles from the plasma produced in the sun. This solar plasma gets caught in the upper atmospheres of Earth and causes green or red glowing clouds to be visible at certain times of the year in the night sky.

**Fluorescent light** bulbs are not like regular light bulbs. That is because inside the long tube is a gas. When **electricity** flows through the tube, we see a light made of plasma because electricity acts as an energy source that charges the gas. The charged and excited atoms create glowing plasma inside the bulb: the energy provided by electricity helps to ionize the gas molecules freeing their electrons. Florescent lights, unlike the stars, are low-temperature plasmas.

**Neon signs**, like fluorescent lights, are also glass tubes filled with gas. When light is turned, electricity flows through the tube charging the gas and creating plasma inside of the tube. The plasma glows a certain color depending on what type of gas is inside the tube. Neon (Ne) gas and many other noble gases such as helium (He), Argon (Ar), and Xenon (Xe) are all typically used in signs. Like, florescent light bulbs, neon signs are also low-temperature plasmas.

**Lightning** strikes occur when air (a gas) changes from a gas to plasma. Lightning is also a discharge of **static electricity**. Static electricity is nature's way of making opposites attract. That is because positively charged particles are attracted to negatively charged particles. Inside the cloud, water molecules rub together and separate into positive and negative charges. The lightweight positive ice particles gather at the top of the cloud while the heavier negative water particles settle at the bottom. The buildup of negative particles at the bottom of the cloud becomes so great that the charge jumps to the ground where particles are positively charged. This jump emits a giant spark or lightning bolt. The energy released from the static electricity causes the gas molecules in the cloud to change <u>temporarily</u> to plasma. Because plasma is attracted by the magnetic pull of the Earth, lightning is direct down to the surface of Earth. However, once it strikes the Earth, it does not have enough energy to remain as plasma.

# Experiments in Electricity in Matter

Now that you've learned how electricity flows through and exists in matter, it's time to try some experiments that deal with this concept. Since the amount of energy to change matter to plasma is not safe to experiment with at home, you can try some safe experiments that deal with electricity and plasma.

**1. Which household materials are conductors and which are insulators?**

**Research:** Briefly research how electricity flows through a circuit. Think about what you already know about materials that are conductor and that are insulators.

**Hypothesis:** Write your own educated guess as a statement that answers the question.

**Materials:** four (4) pieces of coated electrical wire with alligator clips on each end of wires; a D battery; small light bulb; household items (paper clip, toothpick, a glass cup or container, aluminum foil, banana, soda can, water bottle, copper penny, nail, dental floss, plastic comb); bulb holder (optional); D battery holder (optional); paper and pencil

**Procedure:**

o List all of the household items on your paper and next to each one predict if it is a conductor or an insulator.

o Create a simple closed circuit by connecting two wires to the battery and light bulb. Connect the wires by clipping the alligator clip of one wire to the positive post of the battery and the other end to the metal contact (bottom tip) of the bulb. Then, attach the alligator clip of a second wire to the bottom or negative side of the battery by using masking tape or simply holding the clip in place. If the circuit is correct or "closed", a complete path is created, and the bulb will light.

o Test each household item to see if it is a conductors or an insulators. Test one item at a time by making it part of the circuit. Disconnect one alligator clip from the bulb and attach the clip to the test item. Then, connect another wire to the test item and then back to the bulb. If the bulb lights, then the test item is a conductor. If the bulb does not light, then the test item is an insulator.

**Observations:**

o List all the items you are testing on a piece of paper. Record whether each item is a conductor (bulb lights up) or an insulator (bulb does not light up).

**Conclusion:**

o Was your hypothesis correct? Look at your list of predictions. Which were correct?

o How do you know? What evidence supports your conclusion?

## 2. What can static electricity do?

**Research:** Briefly research or think about what you already know about static electricity around your home.

**Hypothesis:** Write your own educated guess as a statement that answers the question.
**Materials:** a dry plastic comb; a sink with a faucet: a head of dry, clean human hair

**Procedure:**

o Slowly turn on the faucet until there is a thin stream of water flowing (about 1 cm. in diameter).
o Brush the plastic comb through the dry, clean human hair 10-15 times.
o Slowly bring the comb close to the flow of water without touching the water (the stream of water should bend towards the comb).
o Repeat 3-5 times by brushing the same person's or another person's hair.

**Observations:**

o Describe what happened each time you brought the comb to the flow of water.

**Conclusion:**

o Was your hypothesis correct?

o How do you know? What evidence supports your conclusion?

## 3. Can energy or electricity occur naturally?

**Research:** Briefly research closed circuits and what potatoes have in them that produces an electric charge.

**Hypothesis:** Write your own educated guess as a statement that answers the question.

**Materials:** one (1) large potato; small light bulb; two (2) copper pennies (or copper nails); three (3) copper wires; two (2) zinc or zinc-plated nails

**Procedure:**

o Cut the potato in half and make a small slit for each penny to fit into.

o Take the 2 copper wires and wrap the end of each one several times around each penny. Do <u>not</u> touch copper wires together.

o Push one penny into each slits on the potato. Each potato now has one penny in it with a wire connected.

o Take the third piece of copper wire and wrap it around the flat end of one zinc nail. Push the sharp end of the nail into one half of the potato about ½ inch from the penny. Do not allow the nail to touch the penny.

o Take the wire connected to the penny in the half of potato with the nail and wrap some of it around the second nail. Stick that second nail into the other potato half. Each potato now has one penny with a wire connected and one nail with a wire connected.

o Use caution when handling the wires to close the circuit. There will be a small electric charge running through the wires. Hydrogen gas is also a byproduct of the chemical reactions in the potato. So, do not perform the experiment near open flames or strong sources of heat.

o Finally, take the two ends of wire that remain loose (one should be from a penny and the other from a nail), and touch them to the small light bulb. If the circuit is set up correctly, the bulb will light. Some troubleshooting may be necessary to get the bulb to light.

**Observations:**

o Describe what happened when you closed the circuit.

**Conclusion:**

o Was your hypothesis correct?

o How do you know? What evidence supports your conclusion?

**4. How is lightning made?**

**Research:** Briefly research or think about what you already know about how lightning is produced.

**Hypothesis:** Write your own educated guess as a statement that answers the question.

**Materials:** a day that is cool (outside temperature is less than 75°F) and with low-humidity (less than 45% humidity); one (1) rubber glove; one (1) plastic fork; aluminum foil; a wood or plastic cutting board; a Styrofoam plate; a clean, dry head of human hair or wool fabric; a darkened room (with some light so as to see the materials and read the procedure)

## Procedure:

o Fold the aluminum foil into a flat, square shape around the plastic fork so that it looks like a spatula. Round the corners slightly.

o Put on the rubber glove and use the gloved hand to rub the Styrofoam plate on your hair or onto the wool. Rub ten times.

o Place the plate onto the cutting board. Use the gloved hand to pick up the aluminum foil covered fork.

o Touch and hold the aluminum foil part of the fork to the plate. Then, touch the foil with your other ungloved hand. Last, pull the fork up from the plate, and touch the plate again.

## Observations:

o Describe what happened each time you touched your ungloved hand to the aluminum foil on the fork?

## Conclusion:

o Was your hypothesis correct?

o How do you know? What evidence supports your conclusion?

**5. What can be done safely with a plasma ball?**

**Research:** Briefly research or think about what you already know about plasma balls and florescent lights.

**Hypothesis:** Write your own educated guess as a statement that answers the question.

**Materials:** plasma ball (any size); florescent light (tube type, not coil type)

**Procedure:**

o Turn on the plasma ball.

o Slowly bring the fluorescent bulb close to the plasma ball.
o See how much you can control the bulb is lit with your hand. Make the light inside the florescent bulb fade or brighten as you pull the light from and towards the plasma ball.

**Observations:** Describe what happened each time you brought the florescent bulb towards and then away from the plasma bulb.

**Conclusion:**

o Was your hypothesis correct? Look at your list of predictions. Which were correct?

o How do you know? What evidence supports your conclusion?

# Chapter 3 Quiz

**I. Circle the word that correctly completes each statement.**

1. Plasma is the most common type of matter found (on Earth) (in the universe).

2. Electricity (is) (moves through) matter.

3. (A neon sign) (lightning) is a type of static electricity.

4. (Salt water) (rubber) is a conductor.

5. (Plasma) (gases) carry an electric current and generate a magnetic field.

6. When enough energy in the form of heat is added to a gas, it becomes (plasma) (liquid).

7. Plasma and gases (have) (do not have) definite shape, so the atoms spread out evenly and take on the shape of their container.

8. (Liquid) (plasma) does not have a neutral charge like the other states of matter because they are both positively charged (+) and negatively charged (-).

**II. True or False: Answer each of the following questions by writing a T for true or F for false.**

9. Neon signs and florescent light bulbs get very hot. _____

10. The Northern Lights are caused by plasma due to solar winds. ____

11. Glass is a conductor and does not conduct electricity. ____

12. When a gas is ionized sufficient energy is provided to free electrons from atoms or molecules, so both ions and electrons now exist together. ____

13. Protons carry a negative charge. Electrons carry positive charge. ____

14. Plasma is not commonly found on Earth in nature. It is more commonly found as

man-made materials. ___

15. Hydrogen and helium are common gases found in neon signs.___

16. Electricity is the 4th state of matter. ___

**III. Give two examples of each term.**

17. plasma _____ _____

18. static electricity _____ _____

19. conductor _____ _____

20. insulator _____ _____

# Chapter 4: Organisms

## Living, Non-Living and Dead

All things on Earth fit into three categories, living, non-living and dead. **Living things** are made out of **cells,** while **non-living** things are composed of molecules and atoms. Anything is considered **dead** if it was once living.

What's the difference between the three? Biologist use several factors to determine is something is living, such as the ability to reproduce, eat, grow, produce waste and so on. Non-living things like light, rocks, minerals and water are made up of molecules, atoms or particles, not cells. Non-living things cannot make more of themselves and cannot do the complex things that living things with cells do. **Dead** things use to be able to but no longer can reproduce, eat, grow, produce waste, etc. With animals, it is easy to know when they're dead. Scientists call a dead animal a carcass. But, plants can be dead too such as wood, a fallen leaf or a dried flower.

List 5 living things: _____ , _____ , _____ ,
_____ , _____

List 5 non-living things: _____ , _____ ,
_____ , _____ , _____

List 5 dead things: _____ , _____ , _____
, _____ , _____

# Cells: The Building Blocks of Life

Now that you understand the difference between living, non-living and dead, let's explore living things in greater detail. Living things are animals, plants, fungi, bacteria, and protists. **Cells** are what living things are composed of. Cells are said to be the **building blocks of life**. That is because the cell is the basic unit of life. All life on Earth is composed of cells. Unlike atoms and molecules, cells have the unique ability to **reproduce** and multiply (make more of themselves).

Biologists call living things **organisms**. There are several million organisms on Earth. Scientists have classified and named around 1.5 million organisms. Some organisms are made up of just one cell and are called **single-celled organisms**. Bacteria, algae and amoebae are types of single-celled organisms. Other living things are composed of trillions of cells and are called **complex organisms** such as mammals. There are also organisms that cannot be seen with the naked eye. Scientists call the tiniest organisms **microorganism** because "micro" means extremely small and can only be seen with a microscope.

Because there are so many types of organisms, it makes it challenging for scientists to neatly define the characteristics of organisms. But some general attributes of organisms can be listed, as long as we remember that not every characteristic is true about every organism. For example, plants are living things, but without muscles and a nervous system they do not have the ability to move on their own.

**Characteristics of living things:**

- made up of one or more cells
- need food, water and air to survive
- take in energy (like food or the sun) and use it to grow
- may have the ability to move on their own
- reproduce (make more of themselves)
- respond and adapt to their environment

One other very important characteristic about all organisms is they can maintain **homeostasis**. When there are external (outside) changes such an increase or decrease of temperature, it is homeostasis that controls or regulates cells of the organism to balance the external change. Homeostasis allows for an organism to be stable, balanced and function properly. Homeostasis, therefore, gives all living things the ability to maintain their survival. That is why one characteristic of living things is that they can respond and adapt to their environment. Both plants and animals have common ways they respond and adapt to order to maintain homeostasis.

**Examples of homeostasis in animals**:

- curling up
- seeking shade
- panting
- shivering

**Examples of homeostasis in plants:**

- moving towards the sun (like a sunflower)
- buds opening
- becoming dormant during winter

When homeostasis gets unbalanced or is not working properly due to problems within the cells or too much change in the environment, the organism will respond by becoming weak or dying. Remember, any organism that was once alive is considered **dead**. Non-living things cannot be considered dead, because they were never living organisms. Homeostasis does not exist within non-living things made only of atoms, molecules or particles.

# Classification of Organisms

Biologists classify or group organisms in an organized ranking system. This is called **taxonomy**. Taxonomy is a scientific term for organizing, classifying and identifying organisms. A taxonomy places organisms into groups based on similarities. The top of a taxonomy starts with the most broad or general ways organism are the same. As we move down, each group gets smaller and smaller as more similar characteristics are defined.

The figure below shows the **taxonomy of organisms** and how humans fit into each category:

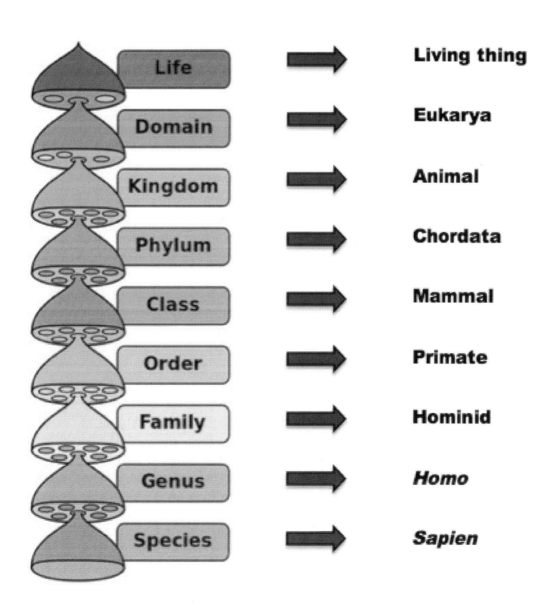

| | |
|---|---|
| Life | Living thing |
| Domain | Eukarya |
| Kingdom | Animal |
| Phylum | Chordata |
| Class | Mammal |
| Order | Primate |
| Family | Hominid |
| Genus | *Homo* |
| Species | *Sapien* |

What Kingdom are humans part of?_____

What Class are humans part of?_____

What Order are humans part of?_____

Do you know any other animals in the same Order as humans?_____

When learning about organisms, it is most helpful to look at **Kingdoms**. These are not the type of kingdoms ruled by kings and queens in castles, but the way all living organisms are classified. Most commonly biologists group all living things into five Kingdoms. Each Kingdom is organized by the organisms cell structure, the way it gets energy, the way it moves, and how it reproduces. The five Kingdoms are:

- **Animalia**-animals
- **Monera**-bacteria
- **Fungi**-things like mushrooms
- **Protista**-molds and algae
- **Plantae**-mosses, ferns and flowering plants

So you may be wondering what the purpose is of all this grouping and classifying. First, it allows biologist to better understand patterns found in nature among organisms. It also shows how organisms are related and what makes them both similar and different. Another reason is it allows us to trace the evolution of plants and animals as well as their extinction.

## Bacteria vs. Viruses

You have probably heard that bacteria and viruses make you sick. While it is true that both bacteria and viruses can cause illness and disease, bacteria and viruses are not both considered living things. Though both have the ability to multiply or make more of themselves, they do so in different ways. Bacteria are indeed a type of organism because their cells survive and multiply on their own without any outside help. Viruses, however, are not considered by scientists to be living organisms. That is because viruses need a **host** to survive. That means a virus can only multiply inside <u>cells</u> of an organism. If a virus invades the cells of an organism, the organism is said to be **infected** or have an **infection.** Viruses can infect all types of life forms, from <u>animals</u> and <u>plants</u> to bacteria. Viruses are all considered harmful to whatever organism they infect. All viruses are also called **pathogens** and all pathogens cause harm to their host. Bacteria, on the other hand, can be both harmful and helpful to other organisms. Some bacteria can causes illnesses such as salmonella and E. coli, which are both food born illnesses (types of food poisoning). But there are many important and helpful or "good bacteria" called **probiotics**. Probiotics are found naturally inside your digestive system and are necessary for your body to properly digest food. Good bacteria also exists in soil and aid in plant growth.

The Venn Diagram below shows the ways bacteria and viruses are both similar and different:

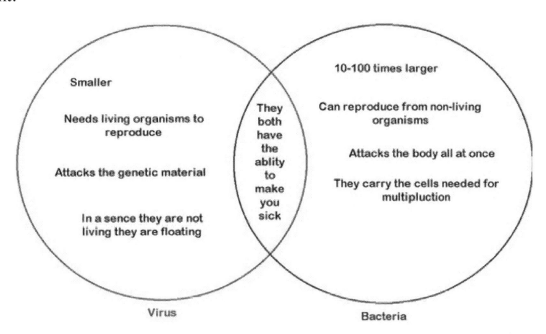

## Looking at Cells

You have learned that all **organisms** are made of cells. Every cell holds all of the equipment necessary for an organism to survive on Earth. It's important to then know that all cells are **organized**. The words **organism** and **organized** both come from the word "organ" which means a fully functional unit. Cells are made up of many organized parts, each with a special function. Cells are unique to each organism. Complex organisms, like plants and animals, have cells that are different from each other. Single-celled organisms and microorganisms have cells that are quite different compared to complex organisms. What all cells have in common though is a **membrane**: a protective wall that holds all the stuff inside the cell and keeps harmful things from getting in.

Complex organisms such as plants and animals have special types of cells that are called **eukaryotes**. Both plant and animal cells have an important common featured called a **nucleus**. The nucleus is like the brain of a cell because it controls such things as eating, movement, growth and reproduction. Another important part of plant and animal cells are the **mitochondria**. Scientists call the mitochondria the batteries or "powerhouses of the cell". They are like teeny tiny digestive organs and are composed of organelles that take in nutrients, break them down, and create energy for the cell. The process of creating cell energy is known as **cellular respiration**.

Plants have a unique feature that animals cell do not. Plant cells have what is called chloroplast. **Chloroplast** is the green part of plants. It is within chloroplast that plants convert the energy of the sun into sugar. These sugars give the plant its own food for it to grow. This process is called **photosynthesis**. Every green plant you see is working to convert the energy of the sun into sugars. Animals then eat the plant, given them energy to grow. In addition, the byproduct of photosynthesis is oxygen that animals use to ,breathe. Yes, plants provide not only food for themselves, but also the food and oxygen for all the animals on Earth, including humans! It is because of what happens in the **chloroplast** during the **process of photosynthesis** that makes plants the basis for life on Earth.

In the figure below, you can also see that animal cells are round or oval while plant cells are box like. The figure also shows the difference between the two types of eukaryote cells:

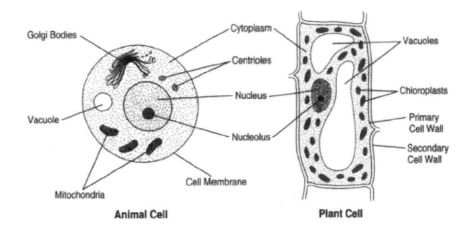

Animal Cell          Plant Cell

List 3 complex organisms that have **eukaryote** cells:

_____, _____, _____

Single-celled organisms have a special type of cell called **prokaryotes**. These cells are very simple, but amazing. It is important to know that prokaryotes do not have a nucleus. All their information is clumped together, floating around inside the cell. Most **bacteria** are prokaryotes and are very, very small. Those that can only be seen with a microscope are called microorganism. These cells were the first types of cells on Earth and were the only living things for about 3 billion years. There are far more prokaryotes on Earth than other type of cells. In fact, there are around ten times more prokaryotes on a human than there are human cells. The figure below shows a single prokaryote.

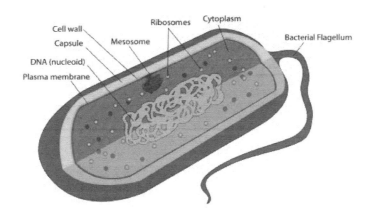

List 3 single-celled organisms that have **prokaryote** cells:

_____, _____, _____

# DNA

How exactly is a cell able to multiply or reproduce? Inside every cell is all the information or the code necessary for the cell to make more of itself. Inside every cell, there are two long chains that twist around each other called **deoxyribonucleic acid** (one type of nucleic acid) also known as **DNA**. The twisting, spiral ladder shape of a strand of DNA is called a **double helix**. That is because every double helix is made up of pairs (a set of two), giving it a ladder shape. Every organism on Earth has a different number and order of base pairs. So, every organism has its own unique DNA.

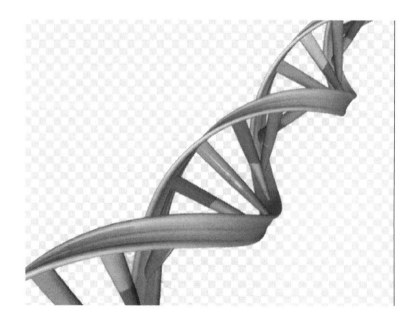

In complex organisms that have eukaryote cells, the DNA is stored in the nucleus. In single-celled organisms (prokaryotes), because they have no nucleus, the DNA floats around inside the cell.

Every time a cell divides (to make more of itself), the spiral ladder winds and unwinds so that the nucleic acid chain can duplicate itself. This duplication process is called **replication.** Life continues for each organism because of the amazing processes that happens inside each cell.

## Cells Within Organism's Systems

Cells go through a duplication process called replication, but do not endlessly go on multiplying. Otherwise, you would continue grow indefinitely. We know that cells are the building blocks of life. That means cells replicate first to form tissue, which then group together to form organs. Organs then form systems and many different systems create a complete organism. Cell tissue constantly need replaced within an organism. But because of homeostasis, cells will only replicate when necessary. Your skin is a good example of this. The top layers of tissue in your skin are constantly flaking off and being replaced by new tissue. But, your body only produces enough cells to replace old, damaged cells.

# Experiments with Organisms

Now that you understand what organisms are and the characteristic of their cells, let's try some experiments that show you some of the processes of organisms.

## 1. How to tell if something is living, non-living or dead?

**Research:** Briefly research or think about what you already know about living, non-living and dead things.

**Hypothesis:** Write your own educated guess as a statement that answers the question.
**Materials:** a rock; any non-poisonous insect; a stick or leaf that's fallen from a tree; a potted plant; paper and pencil

**Procedure:**
o List each item (rock, insect, stick/leaf, plant) on the paper. Study each item listed in materials one at a time.

o Using the *Characteristic of Living Things* list, decide if each item is living, non-living or dead. Use list to provide evidence for your decision:
**Characteristics of living things:**

- made up of one or more cells
- need food, water and air to survive
- take in energy (like food or the sun) and use it to grow
- may have the ability to move on their own
- reproduce (make more of themselves)
- respond and adapt to their environment

**Conclusion:**

o Was your hypothesis correct?

o How do you know? What evidence supports your conclusion?

## 2. What are the parts of a cell?

**Research:** Briefly research the parts of a eukaryote animal or plant cell to create a 3-D model.

**Materials:** any household and/or craft materials of your choice to create model (cereal, balloons, gummy worms, mints, fruit slices, dried fruit, matches, gum balls, peanuts, rope licorice, jelly beans, sesame seeds, other candies, toothpicks, clay, beads, pipe cleaners, Styrofoam ball.

**Procedure:**

o Using an image of the type of cell you want to make, plan and collect the materials you will use to build your 3-D model.

o Put together the model.
o Label each part.

Example:

## 3. Can I see My DNA?

**Research:** Briefly research what human DNA looks like.

**Hypothesis:** Write your own educated guess as a statement that answers the question.
**Materials:** smallest size paper cups; one (1) cup strong saltwater solution;

clear or light colored liquid dish soap; a few drops of pineapple juice; 1 (one) wood skewer ; rubbing alcohol (91-percent isopropyl alcohol works best); narrow container with a lid or a test tube with a stopper (clean, dry); freezer

**Procedure:**

o 24 hours before you start, place the alcohol in the kitchen freezer. It won't freeze, but it needs to be ice cold prior to the experiment.

o Take a large mouthful of salt water and vigorously swish it around in your mouth like mouthwash for at least 2 minutes. It is helpful if you scrape the insides of your cheeks with your teeth, but do not make your cheeks bleed as you want to get DNA from the inside of your cheeks, not your blood.

o Spit the salt water and cheek cell solution into one small paper cup. Pour solution into the test tube or narrow container until it is approximately one-third full.

o Slowly add liquid dish soap until the container is half full. Put on the lid and mix contents by gently rocking the container back and forth and upside down several times. Be gentle, to avoid causing bubbles.

o Add a few drops of pineapple juice. Repeat the gentle mixing from last step.

o Carefully add cold alcohol from the freezer by removing the lid from the cheek cell solution and tilting the container in one hand. Using your other hand, very slowly pour a small amount of rubbing alcohol down the inside of the jar so that the alcohol is floating on top of the cell solution. Then, level the container back to its upright position and set aside for 1 minute.

o After a minute has past, look closely where the alcohol layer is floating on top of the cheek cell solution. A white gooey material should be suspended between the layers of liquids. Use the skewer to carefully wind the white material and lift it out of the container.

o Observe the white gooey material which is your DNA.

**Observations:** Describe what the white material you collected (your DNA) looks like.

**Conclusion:**

o Was your hypothesis correct?

o How do you know? What evidence supports your conclusion?

**4. Under what conditions do molds grow (replicate) best?**

**Research:** Briefly research or think about what you already know about mold and fungus.

**Hypothesis:** Write your own educated guess as a statement that answers the question.
**Materials:** five (5) baby food jars with lids; two (2) cups of hot water: one (1) packet of unflavored gelatin; cotton string; masking tape; permanent marker

**Procedure:**
o To ensure that your mold will grow from the spores you collect and not from the jar

itself, you need to sterilize the jars. With the help of a adult, clean each jar with hot soapy water, rinse with boiling water, then let the jars air-dry. Also, boil the lids in water for at least five minutes.

o Next, add two cups of water to the packet of gelatin and mix until dissolved. Pour the gelatin mixture into each baby food jar so that each jar is half-full. Put aside the leftover gelatin for later use. The gelatin will be the energy or food for the mold organisms grow due to the high protein content.

o One jar will be the "Control" jar (A control is the standard of comparison in any science experiment. Since it has been sterilized, it allows you to compare changes happening in the other jars that will grow mold.) Place the lid on one of the jar label it "Control" with the masking tape and marker.

o Next, cut four, 8 inch pieces of cotton string and dip each string into the leftover gelatin.

o Drag each gelatin-covered string around different areas of your house, like the cat's litter box, a toilet seat, the shower floor, the garbage can, the kitchen counter, the kitchen sponge, and your favorite stuffed animal.

o Last, place each string into the gelatin solution labeling each jar with the place from which you collected spores. Place a lid on each jar and place in a warm area.

o Each day, record (using pictures and/or words) the changes to each gelatin jar. Do this for up to one week.

**Observations:** Describe what happened over the course of a week in each jar. Which area in your home grew the most mold spores when exposed to the warmth and protein in the gelatin?

**Conclusion:**

o Was your hypothesis correct?

o How do you know? What evidence supports your conclusion?


**5. Why do living things need to keep homeostasis?**

**Research:** Briefly research or think about what you already know about living things ability to keep homeostasis. What benefit does this provide an organism?

**Hypothesis:** Write your own educated guess as a statement that answers the question.
**Materials:** 5-10 ants; a glass jar with a metal lid; cold water; a hairdryer

**Procedure:**

o Catch 5-10 black ants (not red ants as they bite). Place them in the jar and put on the lid.

o Place the jar in about ½ inch of cold water. Immediately begin blowing warm air on just the lid of the jar using a hair drier.
o Observe and record what the ants do (they will go towards the warm lid and away from the cold bottom).

**Observations:** Describe the ant's behavior when you placed the jar in cold water and began warming the lid.

**Conclusion:**

o Was your hypothesis correct? How is this an example of homeostasis?

o How do you know? What evidence supports your conclusion?

# Chapter 4 Quiz

**I. Use each of the following vocabulary words to make each statement correct:**

| double helix | mitochondria | chloroplast | eukaryote | replication |
| --- | --- | --- | --- | --- |

1. _____ are the battery of powerhouse of cells because they provide energy for the cell.

2. Complex organisms that have _____ cells that contain a nucleus.

3. A spiral ladder of DNA that cells use to replicate is called a _____.

4. _____ is process of cell division that allows a cell to make more of themselves.

5. _____ is the green part of plants.

**II. In the list below, circle the word if it is an organism and cross out the word if it is a non-living thing.**

6. water

7. mold

8. insects

9. a fire

10. wind

11. flowers

12. the sun

13. an uncooked egg

14. a seed

15. crystals

16. bacteria

17. mushrooms in the ground (not at the grocery store)


**III. Think like a scientist. Answer each question in 1-2 complete sentences.**

18. Why are viruses not considered organisms or living things?

19. How are plant cells different from animal cells?
20. What evidence can you use to prove a cat is an organism?

# Chapter 5: Light

## The Importance of Light

Light seems so simple. It is all around us every day. Light allows us to see. The sun provides light during the day. Lamps and fires provide light during the night. The stars and moon are also a source of light. But light is actually very complex and very important.

The most important type of light is that from the **sun**. The sun's light not only allows us to see, it also allows life to exist on Earth. Sunlight provides warmth and energy that both plants and animals use to grow. Plants use light's energy in a process called photosynthesis, which allows a plant to create the sugars necessary for growth. Animals then eat the plants, allowing the animal to grow. But what is light?

List 3 reasons why light from the sun is important:

1. _____

2. _____

3. _____

## Light is Energy

All light is **energy**. Light is not matter. It has no mass and no electric charge. Light is made of tiny particles called **photons**. Photons travel in a straight path. All light moves in a  straight, wave-like pattern, a bit like how waves travel across a lake or ocean. There are various wavelengths of light. The various wavelengths make up what is called the **electromagnetic spectrum**. Each type of wavelength has its own frequency (size and length), which is calculated in **hertz** (Hz).

Humans can only see light within a certain range of wavelengths and frequency. This range is called the **visible spectrum.** Sometimes the visible spectrum is called **white light**. There are a many non-visible wavelengths that we cannot see such as radio waves, microwaves, infrared rays and X-ways. But even though we can't see these non-visible waves they all have a wide variety of uses in science and technology.

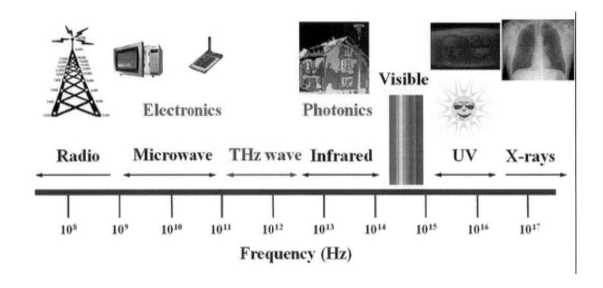

When we compare different types of light on the electromagnetic spectrum, the wavelengths get smaller and closer together as we move up the spectrum. That is because the smaller the wavelength, the greater the energy the light has. For example, X-rays waves and gamma rays have a much greater amounts of energy compared to radio waves. So, X-rays and gamma rays travel is much closer to gather waves than radio waves,

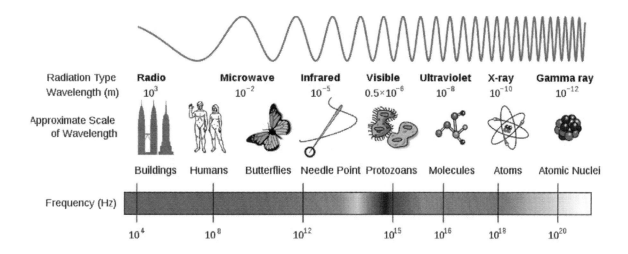

| Radiation Type | Radio | Microwave | Infrared | Visible | Ultraviolet | X-ray | Gamma ray |
|---|---|---|---|---|---|---|---|
| Wavelength (m) | $10^3$ | $10^{-2}$ | $10^{-5}$ | $0.5 \times 10^{-6}$ | $10^{-8}$ | $10^{-10}$ | $10^{-12}$ |
| Approximate Scale of Wavelength | Buildings | Humans | Butterflies | Needle Point | Protozoans | Molecules | Atoms | Atomic Nuclei |
| Frequency (Hz) | $10^4$ | $10^8$ | $10^{12}$ | $10^{15}$ | $10^{16}$ | $10^{18}$ | $10^{20}$ |

You may have noticed that the visible light portion of the spectrum is a rainbow. That is because within the visible spectrum are all the colors that together make up visible light or white light. When we see ordinary daylight, it appears white or colorless, but it contains all the wavelengths of the visible spectrum in equal amounts. Each wavelength is a different color of the rainbow.

There is a clever device or acronym that helps you remember the order of the visible light spectrum that humans can see. The acronym is "ROY G. BIV" Roy is not a real guy, just a way to help remember that the order is:

R (red)

O (orange)

Y (yellow)

G (green)

B (blue)

I (indigo)

V (violet)

Red has the longest wavelength while violet has the shortest. Scientists say that red is the least energetic and violet is the most energetic of the visible spectrum. In the figure below, you can see how each color wavelength in the visible light spectrum gets progressively smaller:

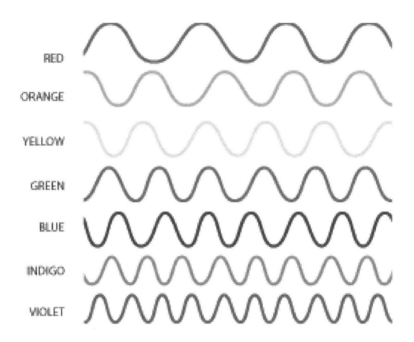

Which type of wavelength is the longest (farthest apart)?_____

Which type of wavelength is the shortest (closest together)?_____

## Speed of Light

Light moves extremely fast. In fact, it moves at the fastest known speed in the entire universe. Since space is a vacuum (lacking air and substance), light has nothing to slow it down. The speed at which light travels is

186, 282 miles per second!! What does that mean? Well, the sun is almost 93 million miles from the Earth and it takes only about seven or eight minutes for light from the sun to get to Earth. And, it takes only about one and half seconds for light to travel from the moon to the Earth. When light travels through matter, like air, water or glass, it does slow down a little, but is still moving very fast. Scientists call the slowing of light as it travels through matter **refraction**. When light is refracted through matter, it also bends.

## Refraction vs. Reflection

Rainbows are a type of **refraction**. That is because visible light or white light is being slowed down as it travels through raindrops in the air. The raindrops act like a **prism**. A **prism** takes in visible light on one side, and because the different colors travel through the prism at different speeds, it cause them to refract or bend at different angles and into all the colors of the visible spectrum. Prisms are often made of triangular shaped glass or crystal. Quite simply, rainbows and prisms separate white light into its colors: red, orange, yellow, green, blue, indigo and violet.

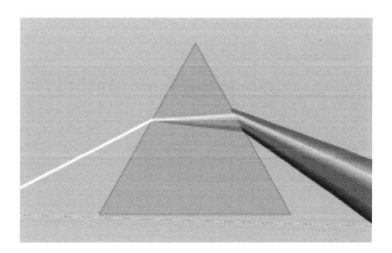

List two other examples of refraction: _____, _____

**Reflection** is another important aspect of light. Reflection is when light hits an object and bounces off. Mirrors are a common type of reflection. But other things reflect such as ponds, the ocean and the moon. Yes, the moon is reflection of the sun's light: the moon does not produce its own light. How well an object reflects depends upon how flat or even the surface is. The rougher the surface, the more the light scatters. And, the more smooth and flat the surface, the better the light bounces off it at equal angles.

List two other examples of reflection: _____, _____

# Light Bulbs

Light from the sun is not the only form of light. Man-made light is a common, everyday necessity. That is due to the invention of the light bulb. Thomas Edison is to thank for that!

There are two common types of light bulbs, the **incandescent lamp** and the **florescent lamp**. The simplest one (invented first by Thomas Edison) is the incandescent lamp. It consists of a clear glass casing, two stiff wires leading up from the base, and a coil of smaller wire made of tungsten called the filament. When electricity to the lamp is turned on, the filament gets hot; so hot that it glows, giving off light. So that filament does not burn up, a mixture of argon and nitrogen gases are pumped into the glass casing. The florescent lamp is much more efficient. It generates light by sending an electrical discharge through an ionized gas: a florescent lamp is a type of man-made plasma.

List 3 other examples of man-made light sources:

_____, _____, _____

# Experiments with Light

## 1. How can I harness the light energy from the sun?

**Research:** Briefly research or think about how to harness the sun's energy and what the sun provides for life on Earth.

**Hypothesis:** Write your own educated guess as a statement that answers the question.
**Materials:** a cylindrical oatmeal box; a sharp knife; aluminum foil; one (1) hot dog; a wooden skewer; an outdoor thermometer; a cooking thermometer; a hot day (at least 75°F)

## Procedure:

o Have an adult cut an oatmeal box in half lengthwise. Line half of the box with aluminum foil, shiny side up.

o Make two small holes, just big enough for the skewer on each of the curved sides of the cylinder. The skewer holes need to be high enough that the hot dog does not touch the aluminum foil, but is no more than1 inch above the aluminum foil.

o Take the hot dog cooker outside and measure the temperature every 3-5 minutes with the outdoor thermometer. Once the temperature is get to 85°F inside the cooker, skewer the hot dog in place. Once the internal temperature of the hot dog gets to 165°F (find by poking the cooking thermometer into the hot dog and leaving it for about 30 seconds), you can remove the hot dog and enjoy.

**Observations:** Describe what happened to the hot dog once it was put on the skewer in the cooker.

## Conclusion:

o Was your hypothesis correct? How was the hot dog able to be cooked?

o How do you know? What evidence supports your conclusion?


## 2. How does light travel?

**Research:** Briefly research and/or think about how light travels.

**Hypothesis:** Write your own educated guess as a statement that answers the question.
**Materials:** three (3) index cards; one (1) small piece of modeling clay; a flashlight; a hole punch; a ruler; a table; a dark room; paper and pencil

**Procedure:**

o On each index card, use the ruler and draw lines connecting opposite corners of the card. At the intersection of the two lines, use the hole punch to put a hole in the center of the index cards. Place all the cards on top of each other to make sure the holes are in the same place on all three cards.

o Use a small piece of modeling clay and place the card into the clay to make the card stand up perpendicular to the table. Place the cards so that they stand vertically, in a straight line and at equal distances from each other.

o Place the flashlight at one end of the row of index cards, then turn off the light in the room.

o Move the index cards until the light can be seen through all the holes.

Observe and record your observations.

**Observations:** Record your observations. Describe what the experiment proves about the path light travels (in a straight line).

**Conclusion:**

o Was your hypothesis correct?

o How do you know? What evidence supports your conclusion?

**3. What common objects show light being bent or refracted?**

**Research:** Briefly research or think about what you already know about light refracting. Where have you seen this happen before?

**Hypothesis:** Write your own educated guess as a statement that answers the question.
**Materials:** water; pencil; a clear glass or clear plastic cup

**Procedure:**
o Fill the glass or cup with water so that is approximately 2/3 full.

o Hold the pencil straight up and down and place it in the glass until it touches the bottom. Get at eye level with the glass and record your observation (pencil still looks normal).

o Lean the pencil until it touches the side of the glass. Let the pencil go as it rests on the side of the glass. Make sure the top part of the pencil is still sticking out of the water.

o Get at eye level again with the glass and record your observations (the pencil appears bent).

**Observations:** Describe how the pencil looked when it was straight up and down and when it was leaning.

**Conclusion:**

o Was your hypothesis correct? How does this show refraction?

o How do you know? What evidence supports your conclusion?

## 4. How can visible light (white light) be broken into the visible light spectrum (a rainbow)?

**Research:** Briefly research or think about what you already know about how visible light can be broken into the visible light spectrum and how rainbows form.

**Hypothesis:** Write your own educated guess as a statement that answers the question.
**Materials:** a drinking glass or glass jar; tap water; one sheet white paper; a sunny day

**Procedure:**
o Take the glass and fill it ¾ full with water. Locate a room with ample sunlight. Put a desk or table in front of the window.

o Take the glass of water and place it where the sunlight passes through the glass and onto the paper. The sun will refract (bend) through the glass and form a rainbow on the sheet of paper, breaking the visible light into all the colors (ROY B BIV).

o Next, hold the glass of water at different heights and various angles to see if the rainbow changes shape or size.

**Observations:** Describe the various refraction of light onto the paper.

**Conclusion:**

o Was your hypothesis correct?

o How do you know? What evidence supports your conclusion?

## 5. If a prism separates visible light into colors, what can put colors back together as white light?

**Research:** Briefly research or think about what you already know about the colors of visible light (white light).

**Hypothesis:** Write your own educated guess as a statement that answers the question.
**Materials:** one (1) white paper plate or white cardboard cut into an exact circle with about a 5 inch diameter; a ruler; a geometry compass; one (1) yard of string; red, green and blue crayons or markers; scissors; pencil

**Procedure:**
o If you're using a paper plate, use the compass to draw a circle around the inner edge of the paper plate inside any rippled area around the edge of the plate. Use the scissors to cut out the circle.

o Use a ruler to draw three straight lines from one edge of the plate to the other so that you make three equal pie-shaped sections on the plate. Color one section red, one section green, and one section blue.

o Use your ruler and pencil to mark the point 3 cm to the left of the center of the circle and another point 3 cm to the right of the center of the circle.

o Thread the string through the holes (in one hole and out the other) and tie the ends of the string together to form a loop that passes through the two holes of the plate.

o Move the circle so that it is in the center of the string with equal amounts of string on either side of the circle. Twist the plate around until tight enough that the twisted string meets your fingers holding the string.

o Pull the twisted ends of the string apart fast enough that string unwinds and the circle spins. and observe the colors on the plate.

o Record your observations of what happens to the colors

**Observations:** Describe what happened to the red, blue and green when the circle was spinning (the colors appear white).

**Conclusion:**

o Was your hypothesis correct?

o How do you know? What evidence supports your conclusion?

# Chapter 5 Quiz

**I. Match each definition on the left with the correct animal class on the right.**

1. **visible spectrum**    The slowing and bending of light as it travels through matter such as air or water.

2. **reflection**    Also known as visible light.

3. **photons**    The wavelengths of light humans can see.

4. **electromagnetic**

   **spectrum**    Glass or raindrops that separate white light into its colors.

5. **refraction**    The simplest type of light bulb containing
   filament.

6. **white light**    Light that allows life to exist on Earth.

7. **prism**    The various wavelengths of light.

8. **incandescent lamp**    A light bulb that send electrical discharge
   through an ionized gas.

9. **florescent lamp**          When a light hits an object and bounces off.


10. **sun**          Tiny particles of which light is made.


## II. True or False: Answer each of the following questions by writing a T for true or F for false.


11. Light is energy. _____

12. Light has mass and an electrical charge. ___

13. Humans can see all wavelengths of light.___

14. ROY G. BIV is an acronym for the order of colors in the visible spectrum. ___

15. Reflection is the bending of light as it passes through matter. ___

16. Light moves at the fastest known speed in the universe. ___

17. Ordinary daylight appears white or colorless. ___

18. Gamma rays have the largest (farthest apart) wavelength and least amount of energy. ___


## III. Think like a scientist. Answer each question in 1-2 complete sentences.


19. What would happen to the Earth if there it no long received light from the sun?

20. What's the difference between reflection and refraction?

# Chapter 6: Human Body

The human body is like a complex machine with many parts that work both independently and together. Humans are of course living things. We are complex and multi-cellular organisms. The human body consists of a system of networks that work simultaneously, allowing for human beings to be one of the most successful and intelligent animals on Earth.

## Human Body Systems

There are many **systems** in the human body. Each system is composed of various **organs** that function independently and together to form a functioning human body. There are two ways to study or learn about the human body. The study of the structures (the parts) of the human body is called **anatomy**, while the study of the functions (how it works) is called **physiology**.

There are a total of 78 organs in the human body. Some of the most important or **major organs** of the human body are:

- skin
- brain
- heart
- lungs
- liver
- kidneys
- stomach
- large intestines
- small intestines
- bladder

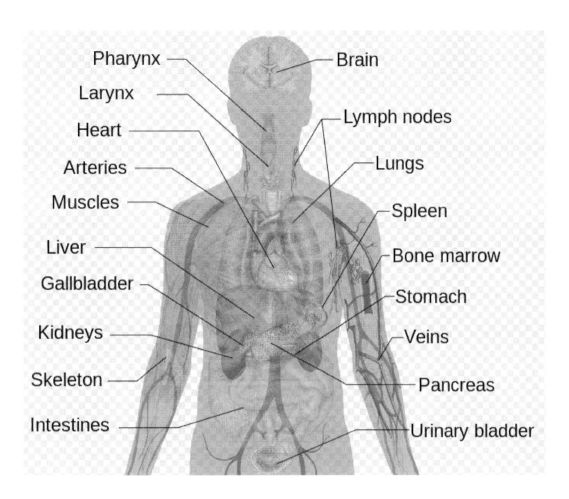

List 3 more organs of the body:

_____, _____, _____

Various organs work together to form organ systems. There are ten major **organ systems** in the bod.  Each one plays a different role in helping the body work, or **function,** correctly.

• **Skeletal and Muscular System** (bones and muscles)

• **Respiratory System** (nose, trachea, and lungs)

• **Circulatory System** (heart, lungs and blood vessels)

• **Digestive System** (mouth, esophagus, stomach and intestines)

• **Nervous System** (brain, spinal cord, and nerves)

• **Urinary System** (bladder and kidneys)

• **Endocrine System** (glands)

• **Immune System** (many types of protein, cells, organs, tissues)

• **Reproductive System** (male and female reproductive organs)

Let's find out the how each system works and what its job is.

## Skeletal and Muscular System

The **skeletal and muscular systems** work together to provide **shape** and **form** for the human body. Bones and muscles **support** and **protect** our bodies, particularly the vital organs such as the brain, heart and lungs. Bones and muscles also allow for the body to **move**.  Without muscles and bones, we would just be blobs on the ground unable to move around.

The **skeletal system** consists of **bones, cartilage**, and **joints**. The **bones** of a skeleton in a museum are dry, hard and dead, but the ones inside a human being are very much alive. Bones of humans grow and change for about the first 25 years of life. Babies are born with about 300 bones that fuse together slowly as the baby grows. An adult skeleton has 206 bones.

Can you name 7 bones? _____, _____, _____,

_____, _____, _____, _____

Some bones provide protection such as the **ribs** and **cranium** (skull). Other bones help you bend and move like the **spine**. There are also long, supportive bones that hold the weight of the body such as the **femur** (top bone of the leg).

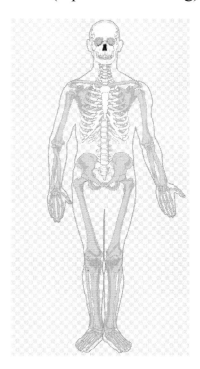

A **joint** is place where two bones meet. Most joints provide movement. But others do not such as the skull bones. One joint that allows for movement is called a **hinge joint**. Your elbows and knees both have hinge joints that allow you to bend and straighten your arms and legs. Hinge joints are just like hinges on a door. Just as doors open one way, hinge joints allow for movement in only one direction. The other type of moving joint is the **ball and socket joint**. These types of joints are found in the shoulders and hips. The round end of one bone fits into a small cup-like area of another bone. Ball and socket joints allow for movement in every direction.

**Cartilage** is a soft, flexible tissue. Cartilage is softer and less rigid than bone but stiffer and less flexible than muscle. Many bones of babies are made of cartilage. As a baby grows the cartilage gradually hardens into bone. Permanent cartilage remains in adults and can be found in the nose, ears and ribcage.

The **muscular system**, just like it sounds, is composed of muscles. Did you know that there are more than 600 muscles in your body? All these muscles have many important jobs:

- allow for movement

- provide heat: keep you warm

- provide stability

You control some of your muscles and can move them on purpose such as when you want to walk or run, pick up an object, and scratch you head. When a muscle is put to work, we say it **contracts**. Other muscles, like your **heart**, do their job for your entire life without you ever thinking about them. The muscles that contract without having to think about it are called **involuntary muscles**. Other involuntary muscles are the bladder and the large and small intestines.

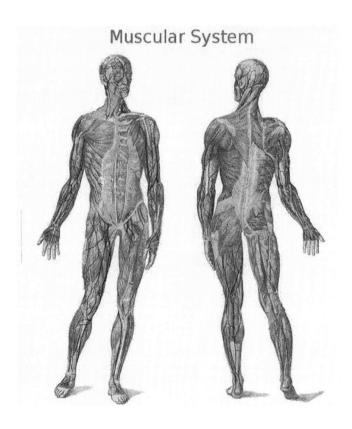

Muscles are all made of a type of elastic tissue called **fibers** that is much like the material in a rubber band. Thousands of small fibers make up each muscle. Muscle fibers work in three different ways. So, there are three different types of muscles in your body:

- **smooth muscle: stomach, bladder and eye muscles**

- **cardiac muscle: the heart**

- **skeletal muscle:** most abundant (about 640 in all), but some you may know are biceps (front of arm), triceps (back of arm), quadriceps (front of leg) hamstring (back of leg), and gluteus maximus (your bottom)

Which type of muscle can you control? _____
Which types of muscles are involuntary muscles? _____, _____

Included in the muscular system are the **tendons** and **ligaments**. The tendons and ligaments are what link the skeletal system with the muscular system. That is because the tendons and ligaments both work with the bones to allow movement. **Tendons** connect muscle to bone, which allows you to move. **Ligaments** connect bone to bone and they help to stabilize the joint (like the knee) they surround.

# Respiratory System

The **respiratory system** is made up of the **nose, trachea, diaphragm** and **lungs**. You know the respiratory system as **breathing**. The lungs are one of the largest organs in the body and are responsible for taking in fresh air (oxygen), getting rid of stale air (carbon dioxide), and allowing humans to speak. The lungs are protected by the ribcage. Just below the lungs is a muscles called the diaphragm that allows the lungs to inhale and exhale. The **trachea** is also known as the windpipe. It is the long tube connecting the mouth and lungs.

The primary job of the respiratory system is to supply the blood with **oxygen**, which is then carried to all parts of the body. Oxygen is essential for the body to function properly, especially the muscles. That is why you breathe faster and harder when you exercise: your respiratory system is working hard to get more oxygen to the muscles.

# Circulatory System

The **circulatory system** is made up of the **heart, lungs** and **blood vessels**. The circulatory system works very closely with the respiratory system. The main job of circulatory system is to carry or **circulate** blood to every cell in the body. To do so efficiently, the blood has to be pumped or pushed throughout the body. And, that is the job of the **heart**: to pump blood. Your blood does not just slosh around your body once it leaves the heart.

Blood moves through many different sized tubes called veins and arteries. Together veins and arteries are called **blood vessels**. All blood vessels are attached to the heart and form what looks a highway system of roads going here, there and everywhere. This system of blood vessels brings blood to and from every body part.

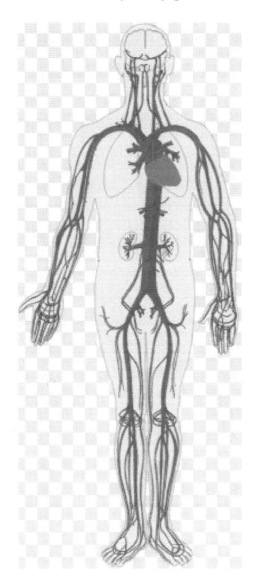

Some appear red and some appear blue. But, why? The **arteries**, which look red, carry clean, oxygenated blood picked up from the lungs away from the heart to the organs and muscles. The **veins**, which look blue, return stale, carbon dioxide filled blood back to the heart. There, the carbon dioxide is push out of the body through the lungs, trachea and nose. Amazingly, it takes less than 60 seconds for the heart to pump blood to every cell in your body. The heart is one strong muscle!

# Digestive System

The mouth, esophagus, stomach and intestines make up the **digestive system**. Digestion is the process of taking food and turning it into energy that every cell of the body needs to survive. So, the purpose of the digestive system is to turn the food you eat into something useful for the body. When you eat, the digestive system processes the nutrients from the food that can be used by the cells to make energy. That means food is fuel.

The process begins in the mouth. The teeth, tongue and **saliva** (spit) begin to break down food into smaller parts. The food travels down a tube called the **esophagus,** which is next to the trachea or windpipe (they are different tubes) and into the stomach. When food or liquid is swallowed, a special flap called the epiglottis closes over the opening of the windpipe to make sure food and liquid does not enter the lungs. In the **stomach,** strong muscles and **gastric acid** mix and churn the food into even smaller parts. Now the food moves into the **small intestine** (which is skinny, but very long) where all the vitamins, minerals, proteins, carbohydrates, and fats are absorbed into the bloodstream for the cells to **metabolize** as energy. First though, the nutrient-rich blood passes through the **liver** that filters out harmful substances and wastes called **toxins**. But, the body cannot process or use all parts of the food we eat. The solid leftover material (poop) passes out of the body through the **large intestine** and then the rectum. The liquids that can't be used (pee) pass out of the body through the **bladder.**

Label the **mouth, esophagus,**

**stomach, small intestines,**

**large intestines, liver,**

and **bladder** on the figure of the

digestive system.

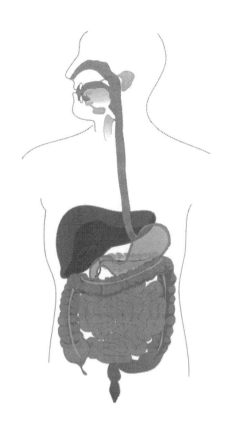

## Nervous System

No need to feel nervous about this system! The **nervous system** is not too difficult to understand. It consists of the **brain, spinal cord**, and **nerves**.

Quite simply, the nervous system is the control center of the human body. All the functions, systems and movements of the body are controlled by the nervous system. The brain receives and interprets information known as **stimuli**. The brain transmits impulses to organs and muscles through the **spinal cord** and the nerves. **Nerves** are the pathways for the information getting to and from the brain. Just like the blood vessels, the nerves run all over the body sending and receiving messages. Your brain is the most important organ in the body. It uses the information and stimuli it receives to organize and direct all of your actions and reactions.

Label the **brain, spinal cord**

**and nerves** on the figure of the nervous system.

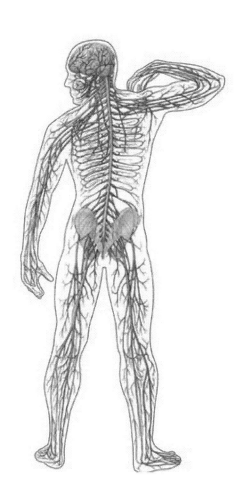

**Urinary System**

Have you heard the term **urine** before? Urine is another word for pee. You know that when you drink, you pee, but there's a lot more to the process than that. The function of the **urinary system** is to filter out excess fluid, waste products and toxins from the bloodstream. The body gets fluid from food and liquids. Much of the fluid gets absorbed by the body to help cells function. What the body can't use or does not need gets expelled as urine. The organs that are involved in this process are **kidneys**, **bladder**, **ureters**, and **urethra**. These make up what is called the **urinary tract**. Each organ in the urinary tract has a unique shape and special job:

- **kidneys**: two bean-shaped organs that act like filters to remove waste from the blood and produce urine
- **ureters**: two thin tubes that transport urine from the kidney to the bladder
- **bladder**: a sac that holds urine until it's eliminated (in the toilet)
- **urethra**: the tube that carries urine from the bladder out of the body during urination

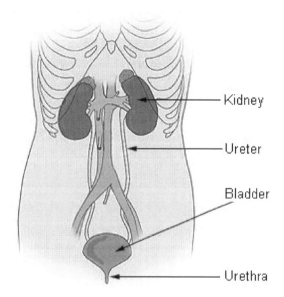

What part of the urinary tract or urinary system holds urine until it is time to go to the bathroom?_____

# Endocrine System

The **endocrine system** is a network of **glands** of various shapes and sizes located throughout the body. The job of the endocrine system is to regulate, coordinate, and control a variety of different body functions by releasing chemicals called **hormones** into the bloodstream. These hormones help control and regulate several things such as:

- **mood**
- **growth**
- **development of male and female reproductive organs responsible for puberty**
- **metabolism** (the ability to digest food into energy)

The "master glands" that controls all the other glands is called the **pituitary gland.** About the size of a pea, it is tucked beneath your brain. The pituitary also controls grow.

The **thyroid gland** is found in the neck. It's shaped like a bowtie. It makes hormones that are important for growth and also helps you stay alert and have a good energy level.

When you are sick or under stress, it is the **adrenal glands** that are called into action. **Adrenaline** is one of the adrenal gland hormones that provide a rush of energy during times of extreme emotion like fear, excitement and anger. A burst of adrenaline is very important for survival.

The larges gland is the pancreas is found in the abdomen (belly). The pancreas makes many hormones, the most of important of which is **insulin**. Insulin controls how much glucose (the sugar that's in your blood) enters the cells of the body. Cells depend on glucose to function: glucose is the fuel on which cells run. Someone whose pancreas does not create proper amounts of insulin are said to have diabetes.

# Immune System

Another word for **immune** is protected.  The **immune system's** function is to fight off sickness and disease. The immune system is made up of a network of cells, tissues, and organs that all work together to protect the body. The germ-fighting cells of the immune system are called **white blood cells** and they are found within blood vessels. Germs are not only fought within the blood stream. Another important part of the immune system is in the **lymph nodes**. The lymph nodes work like filters, removing germs that invade the body that cause illness. Lymph nodes are located on the sides of the neck, behind the knees, in the armpits, and in the groin.

# Reproductive System

The male and female reproductive organs make up the **reproductive system**. These are the parts that most people hide under their swimsuits: reproductive organs include the penis in males and the breasts and vagina in females.  **Reproduction** is how babies are made. The human reproductive system, though sometimes embarrassing to learn about, ensures that humans are able to survive as a species.

# Experiments with the Human Body

Now that you've learned more about the human body machine and all it's systems that work both alone and together, it's time to try some experiments that let you apply this knowledge. These experiments are designed for you to further explore each topic.

## 1. Metabolism: Cells at Work

**Background:** Though yeast is single-celled organism, its cells also use the process of metabolism much like the human body breaks down sugars in food to provide cells energy. One product of sugar being metabolized (getting used for energy) by yeast is the release of a gas called carbon dioxide ($CO_2$). The more carbon dioxide that is released by yeast, the more energy the yeast is using. The amount of carbon dioxide released depends on how much sugar the yeast available.

**Materials:** three (3) twelve-ounce plastic bottles: three (3) balloon; a funnel: a plastic tray: masking tape and marker; one (1) packet of rapid rise active dry yeast; sugar; warm water; measuring cups; a spoon; a measuring tape; paper and pencil

## Procedure:
o Use the masking to label each bottle as follows:
• Bottle #1: Water, ¼ cup sugar, ½ teaspoon yeast

• Bottle #2: Water, ½ cup sugar, ½ teaspoon yeast

• Bottle #3: Water, ¾ cup sugar, ½ teaspoon yeast

o Measure the following amounts for each bottle as labeled ingredient then use the funnel to pour each ingredient into the bottles.

o Measure ½ cup warm water and pour into bottle #1. Immediately place a balloon over the opening of the bottle.

o Repeat pouring ½ cup warm water and placing a balloon over the opening of bottle #2 and the same for bottle #3.

o Gently mix the contents of each bottle gently by swirling each bottle. Then, use the measuring tape to quickly measure the circumference of each balloon.

o Record the circumference of each balloon. Observe each balloon and record.

o Place all three of bottles on the plastic tray and move the trays and bottles to a warm, flat surface (like in front of a sunny window or near a heating vent). Let the bottles sit undisturbed for about one hour.

o After one hour, measure the circumference of each balloon again and record.

**Conclusion:**

o Which bottle released the most gas into the balloon? Why?

(Bottle #3 with the most amount of sugar should have made the balloon expand the most giving it the larges circumference because the yeast had more food (sugar) to metabolize, releasing the most carbon dioxide gas.)

**2. Let's Get Pumping: The Circulatory and Respiratory System at Worth Together**

**Background:** The heart and lungs must work harder to pump oxygen to the muscles during exercise. Also, it very important to make your heart muscle work harder and so exercise is vital to maintaining good health. Exercise that elevates heart rate is the most beneficial to heart and will also increases lung capacity. Heart rate is measured by many times a person's heart beats in a minute. This is called beats per minute (bpm).
**Materials:** a timer, watch or clock that shows seconds; comfortable clothes and shoes for exercise; a jump rope; paper and pencil

**Procedure:**
o Take your pulse when you are calm and have been sitting still for a while to calculate your RESTING heart rate. To do so, lightly place the first two fingers of one hand on your opposite wrist to feel your pulse. You will find your pulse below your thumb at the base of your palm. Pushing too hard will make it difficult to feel your pulse. Do not use your thumb as it has it's own pulse.

o Use the stopwatch to time yourself jumping rope. After one minute of jumping rope, stop the stopwatch and stop jumping. Take your pulse for 10 seconds. Record only how many beats there were in 10-seconds. Later, you will calculate all your bpm's

o Resume the stopwatch and continue jumping rope. Stop again at 2 minutes, 5 minutes, 10 minutes and 15 minutes to take and record your heart rate. Stop at anytime if you feel dizzy or light headed.

o Calculate all bpm's for each interval of exercise (1 min., 2 min., 5 min., 10 min., and 15 min.) and your resting heart rate bmp. To do this, multiply each 10-second pulse reading by 6. For example, if at one minute you counted 16 beats, your bpm would be 96 (16 x 6 = 96).

**Observations:** Describe and record how you felt the longer you jumped rope. Describe what happened to your bpm the more you exercised compared to your resting heart rate.

**Conclusion:**

o Your bmp will have gradually increased as you began to exercise and probably began to level out somewhere around 10 minutes.

## 3. How Handy! Muscles, Tendons and Bones at Work

**Research:** Muscles, tendons (part of the muscular system) and bones (of the skeletal system) work together to all the human body to move. The skeletal muscles in your body (like your hand) shorten or contract when your brain tells them to do so. The muscles inside your forearm have tendons running through that attach at the wrist. These tendons and muscles allow you to bend your fingers and thumb.

**Materials:** A piece of cardboard at least the size of your hand; a pen or pencil; scissors; string; a stapler

**Procedure:**
o Trace the outline of your hand with a pen or pencil on the cardboard. then use the scissors to cut out the shape of your hand.

o Cut the string into five (5) pieces each the length of your hand.

o Tie one piece of string to the tip of each finger and the thumb. Stretch each pieces of string to the base of the palm so that the string is lying flat on the cardboard (not bending the cardboard).

o Using your hand as a model, staple the string to the card at the same points where you have joints in your fingers and thumb.

o Pull each of the strings from the base of the palm.

o Record your observations of what happens to cardboard hand.

**Conclusion:**

o Pulling the string from the palm mimics the movement of the muscles and tendons that bend the finger bones towards the palm.


## 4. The Nervous System at Its Simplest: The Knee Jerk Reflex

**Background:** The knee jerk reflex is tested at a check up with your doctor off. It's quite simple. The doctor hits your knee just below your knee cap WAM!...your leg kicks out automatically. Why? The knee jerk reflex is a monosynaptic reflex (mono means one and synaptic refers to the nerves that deliver information to the brain). Since there is only one single synapse to the nerve to complete the reflex, it takes merely 50 milliseconds between the tap and the leg kick.
**Materials:** a partner (Yep, that's it!)

**Procedure:**
o Have a partner sit one an elevated surface with his or her legs uncrossed so that the legs swing freely without touching the ground.

o Squeeze your fingers and thumb so they are flat and rigid Hit your partners leg (like a semi-forceful karate chop).just below the knee with the pinky side of your hand. Do not use a hammer or other hard device. If you hit just the right spot, the leg will kick out immediately.

o Switch spots and let your partner try it on you.

**Conclusion:**

o The tap below the knee causes a single to be sent to the brain telling the thigh muscle to contract, which then straightens the leg (like when you kick a ball).


## 5. Ball and Socket Joint Exploration

**Background:** Ball and socket joints are found in shoulders and hips of a human body. These joins have a greater range of motion than elbows and knee joints (hinge joints) because they can move in many directions, side-to-side, front to back, and up and down.
**Materials:** one 3 oz. paper cup; clay; craft sticks

**Procedure:**
o Roll enough clay in into a ball so that the diameter of the ball is just slightly smaller

than the diameter of the paper cup.

o Place the clay ball into the paper cup. Then press the end of a craft stick into the clay.

o Rotate the craft stick so the ball moves around inside the cup the same way a ball and socket joint rotates.

o Rotate your arm around (getting your shoulder to move) to see how it moves the same way. Do the same with your leg to feel how your hip moves.

**Conclusion:**

o The model will move the same as your shoulder and hips do. You can also try cupping one hand and making the other into a fist, then placing your fist in the cupped hand, rotate your fist around.

# Chapter 6 Quiz

**I. Write the name of the body system after each description.**

1. Name the body system helps humans turn the food they eat into energy.

_____

2. Name the body system helps humans breathe. _____

3. Name the body system controls other body systems. _____

4. Name the body system provides structure for the body.

_____

5. Name the body system allows us to move. _____

6. Name the body system transports blood and with a pump (the heart).

_____

**II. Answer each question using a few words or short phrases.**

7. What are two body systems that work together? (Examples include the respiratory and circulatory, muscular and skeletal, digestive and circulatory, and nervous and any other system.)

8. Which organ of the nervous system is most important for it to work properly? (Brain.)

9. What can cause harm to one or more body systems? (Injury or disease could disrupt one or more body systems.)

10. Which system is responsible for protecting the body and fighting off germs? (Immune)

11. What are two jobs of the endocrine system? (regulate mood, control growth, regulate male and female organs during puberty, regulate metabolism)

**III. True or False: Answer each of the following questions by writing a T for true or F for false.**

12. The systems of the human body are independent and function on their own. ___

13. There are different three types of muscles. ___

14. Reproduction ensures the survival of humans as a species. __

15. The endocrine system is a network of glands located throughout the body that are all the same shapes and sizes. ___

16. The human body is complex and multi-cellular organism. ___

17. The liver, kidneys and brain all act like a filter to remove waste from the body. ___

18. Excess fluids called urine are stored in the bladder and excreted (when it's time to use the toilet). ____

19. The digestive system processes the nutrients from the food that can be by the cells to make energy, so food is really fuel. ____

20. The "master glands" that controls all the other glands is called the pancreas. ____

# Chapter 7: Life Cycle and Reproduction

An organism is any living thing. All organisms grow and change. Plants, animals and even bacteria all go through a series of stages from the beginning of life until death. This is called a **life cycle**.  Not all life cycles are exactly the same. There are simple life cycles like that of fish, mammals and birds. And there are more complex life cycles of animals that go through a metamorphosis such as amphibians and insects. Plants also go through life cycles that are different from those of animals.

## Fertilization and Reproduction

All living things reproduce. That means they make more of themselves to ensure the survival of their species. In animals, for new life to begin, a male and female must mix their genetic information of their cells. All organisms pass characteristics of themselves to the next generation through their **genes**. A gene is a component of DNA that is passed down from parent to offspring (child). The **genes** in animals come from the male's **sperm** and the female's **egg.** If a female (the mother) and male (the father) of a species get together and mix the sperm and an egg, **fertilization** occurs. The blending of male sperm and female egg form a **zygote**, and a new life has been created. This new life is often referred to as a baby. This process is known as **reproduction**, which allows organisms to make more of themselves.

## Birds

Birds do not give birth to live young. All birds begin their life as an **embryo** inside an egg laid by a female bird (the mother). If a male has **fertilized** an egg, then a baby bird will begin to form and grow inside the egg. Generally, the female (mother) will sit on the eggs to keep them warm until they hatch. The female develops extra blood vessel in her chest that act like a heating pad to keep the eggs warm. The time a bird is developing inside the egg is called **incubation**. Incubation lasts for around 3 weeks.

Next, the egg will begin to **hatch**. The baby bird, called a **chick**, uses a small tooth-like part on its beak to crack the egg's hard shell. The chick wiggles and pushes itself out of the egg. When the chicks hatch, they're called **nestlings**. The nestlings are helpless, so the adult bird continues to sit on the nest for a few days, bringing the hatchlings food so they can grow.

The nestlings inside the nest and become **fledglings**. They can feed themselves but still need their parents. **Fledgling**s leave their parents and the nest at the end of this stage. It takes about three months for a chick to develop into a fledgling and leave the nest.

Once a bird leaves the nest is an **adult**. The adult bird finds its own food and protects itself. Birds do not stay with or return to their parents. At the adult stage, birds begin **courtship**. This is the process of finding a **mate**, a bird of the opposite sex. Next, the male and female birds will build a nest. When the nest is completed, the two birds mates. This is when the male fertilizes the female's eggs, and the life cycle begins again.

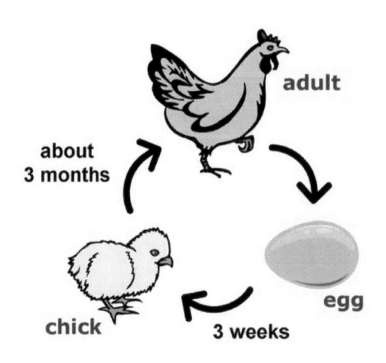

# Humans

The life cycle of a human is similar to that of a bird, but there is one important difference, that is humans give birth to live young. But how the baby is created is very similar to that of birds. Because humans are mammals, they share a similar life cycle to most other mammals.

It begins when a male inserts his penis into the female's vagina. This is called **sexual intercourse** and it allows the male's sperm to mix with a female's egg inside the woman's body: a **zygote** has been formed. The zygote will settle inside the woman's **uterus**. The uterus is often also called the **womb.** The uterus is one of the female productive organs located in the pelvis (hip area) in front of the digestive organs. Here the zygote is now called a fetus. A **fetus** is a developing baby inside a mother. This stage of development takes nine months while the fetus is developing inside the mother until it is ready to be born.

A human baby is born by passing through the woman's vagina. At this stage of development, the **baby** is helpless and depends on its parents to take care of it. Their parents must feed them, change their diapers and carry them anywhere they need to go. As the baby grows and develops, it begins to learn how to move on its own, first by crawling then by walking.

As you know, babies eventually become more independent, learning how to feed themselves, use the toilet, and to speak. The next stage of development is called **childhood**. A child is still dependent on its parents. That is because they have so much to learn.

Around the age of twelve, the next stage of development begins. It is called **adolescence**. There is a great deal of growth during this stage, both physically and mentally. Adolescents become more independent and are capable of doing things by themselves. They also grow a lot, getting taller, heavier and stronger. Also, both the male and female reproductive organs begin to change and develop. This time of change is called **puberty**. During puberty the body is flooded with **hormones** from the pituitary glad that allow the adolescent's reproductive organs to be ready for the next stage of development, called adulthood.

**Adulthood** is when we become responsible for our own actions and no longer rely on their parents to look to care of their needs. Adults have stopped growing. We say they are **mature** or have reached maturity. Adults are physically ready to have babies of their own and start the life cycle again.

# Frogs

Frogs and other amphibians have similar life cycles that are a bit more complex than mammals and birds. That is because they go through a **metamorphosis**, or a complete change in form.

Frogs also begin as a fertilized **egg** (not pictured below). The female lays a large amount of eggs in one big clump in the water. That is because only a small number of the eggs survive and become **tadpoles (figure a)**.

Tadpoles are baby frogs and are the second stage of the frog life cycle. Tadpoles begin as a fish-like creature with only a tail. They eat algae. They also breathe through gills. Over the period of six to nine weeks, the tadpole begins to grow first front legs (figure b) and then back legs (figure c). At about twelve weeks, they shed their tail (figure d). During the last stage as a tadpole their gills change to lungs so they can breathe air. Now they are ready to emerge from the water.

An **adult frog** (figure e) has made a complete metamorphosis from fish-like algae eater that breathes with gills to a four-legged carnivore with lungs. It will lay or fertilize eggs and begin the life cycle all over again.

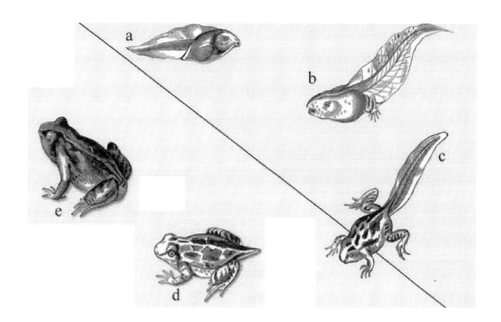

## Bees

Insects, like bees, have a unique life cycle that also involves a **metamorphosis**. The stages in the life cycle of a bee are **egg, larva, pupa** and **adult**.

Only one female in a hive lays eggs. This is called the **queen bee**. She mates with the male drones to fertilize the eggs, and then lays one egg in every cell of the honeycomb. A queen lays about 2000 eggs per day!

The egg immediately begins to grow into a **larva** inside its cell of the honeycomb. Just four days after being laid, the larva hatches into a white legless **larva**. The larva molt (shed their skin) four or five times as they grow. After about nine days, the larva spins a cocoon, much like a caterpillar or moth. This stage of a bee's life cycle is called the

**pupa**.

As a pupa inside the cocoon, the bees develop legs, eyes and wings. After about two weeks, the bee chews its way out and emerges as a fully-grown, mature **adult**, making a complete metamorphosis.

The adult stage is the final stage of in the life cycle of a bee. Most adult bees are worker bees or drone bees. If a new queen bee is born, she will either replace a dying queen or she will leave the colony to start her own, and the starts all over again.

# Plants

Plants, as living things, also go through a life cycle like all organisms do.

Just like animals, plants also are born and grow up and mature into adults. There are three types of plants which scientists group by their life cycles: **annuals, biennials**, and **perennials. Annuals,** like sunflowers and pea plants, have the shortest life cycle of just one year. **Biennial** plants such as pansies have a life cycle of two years. **Perennials,** like daisies, shrubs and trees, have the longest a life cycle of more than two years. All three types of plants, however, follow the same basic stages in their life cycle.

All plants begin as a **seed**. During seed stage, the pod (covering of the seed) protects seed **embryo** inside. A seed is a living thing, but it is **dormant**. That means it is resting, waiting for the right conditions to sprout.  As the seed prepares to sprout, it absorbs water until the roots and small leaves emerge. The sprouting of a seed is called **germination**. Germination is the birth of a plant.

Once the plant has germinated, it is called a **seedling**. During this stage, the plant is small but grows rapidly. It is a baby plant. Soon the plant is big enough that is can absorb enough sunlight and water to begin enter for the **flowering** stage. During the flowering stage, the plant will reproduce in order to make more plants. To reproduce, a plant has to be **pollinated** by the helped by bees and other animals. Just like animals, plants must be **fertilized**. Pollination is the process of pollen (a dust-like material) being transferred from the **anther** (male flower part) to the **stigma** (female flower part) of a plant.

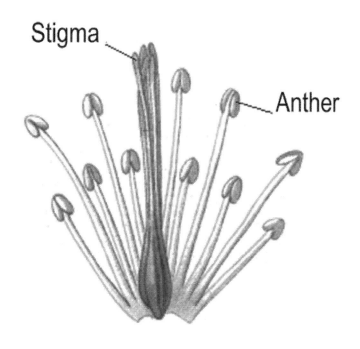

Yes, flowers have both male and female reproductive organs! Some plants fertilize themselves, while others need pollen from another plant of the same type. Once a plant has been pollinated, it begins to produce seeds. The seeds then drop off and fall to the ground, and the life cycle starts all over again.

# The Life Cycle of a Plant

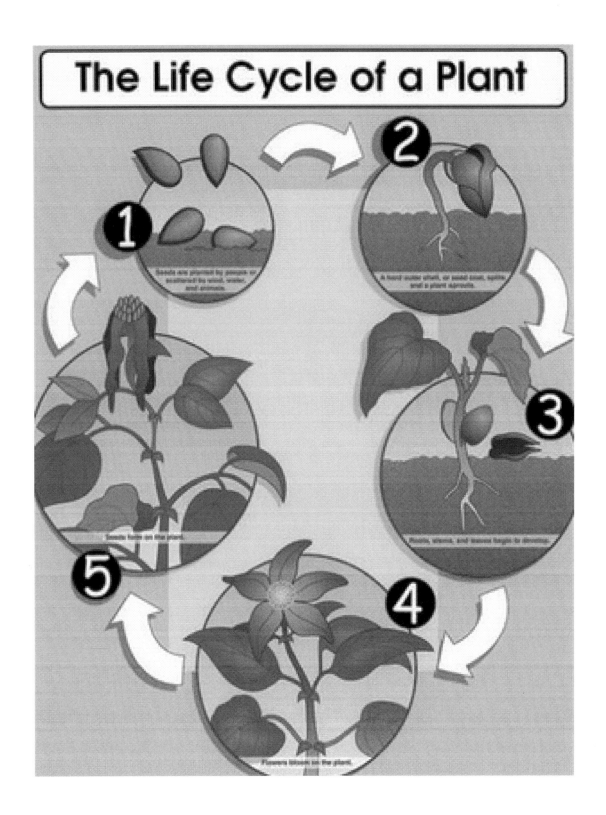

# Experiments with Life Cycles

Now that you've learned how all organisms go through life cycles, you can try some hands-on exploration of various types of life cycles.

## 1. Butterfly Hatchery

• **What you need:** caterpillars; their food source; ventilated container

• **What you do:**

o Collect several caterpillars. To find caterpillars, locate their food source. Lift up various plants' leaves in the spring. Gently pull the caterpillars off and place them in a ventilated jar. You can also purchase caterpillars. If you buy them, read the instructions they come with carefully.

o To care for the caterpillars, you need a container that allows the caterpillars to get air and to move around, such as a small aquarium with a screen lid. Next, add the caterpillars and their food source. Check each day of the food supply needs replaced. Observe how the caterpillar eats.

o After about two weeks, the caterpillars will go to the top of the container, spin a button of silk and hang in a J-shape. Then, they will transform in a chrysalis.

o Once the butterflies emerge, observe how their wings pump up with blood so they can fly. Dissolve sugar into water and place it in a shallow dish inside the container. Observe how the butterfly eats (with a proboscis). After 3-5 days, release the butterflies so they can start the life cycle again.

• **What you have learned**: Use complete sentences to answer the following questions:

o Do caterpillars and butterflies eat the same thing?

o What are the stages of the life cycle of a butterfly?

## 2. Meet the Mealworm

• **What you need:** about 20 large mealworms (NOT king mealworms) from the local pet store; wheat bran or bran meal; a potato, sweet potato, carrot, or apple; clear basin lid or aquarium with lid; paper and pencil

• **What you do:**

o Microwave the package of wheat bran for 1 minute to kill any stray organisms. Pour the bran meal onto the floor of the container so it is 1 inch deep.

o Cut the potato, carrot or apple into ¼ inch cubes. Place one cube in the container. Store the rest in a seal container in the refrigerator.

o Add mealworms to the container and put on the lid. The mealworm can't escape yet, but it will later.

o Each day, see if the potato, apple or carrot needs replenished. Always put the lid back on afterwards.

o Observe the mealworms movements. You can pick one up and examine it.

o Around one week, observe and record the mealworms to shrink and curl into a crescent wax-like shape.

o After about two weeks, observe and record observations comes out of the crescent wax-like shape. At this stage, the organism can escape, so keep the lid on and replenish food source carefully.

o After about three weeks, observe and record the organism. Each day check to see if you can see the life cycle beginning again.

• **What you have learned**: Use complete sentences to answer the following questions:

o What are the stages and characteristics of the mealworm's life cycle?

o What other organisms have a similar life cycle? Why?


### 3. Ant Farm Antics

• **What you need:** a small glass bowl or jar; a glass fishbowl; sand; soil; sugar; water; 20 ants (all from the same colony); cheesecloth; a rubber band; black construction paper; bread crumbs; masking tape

• **What you do:**

o Collect at least 20 ants from the same colony or anthill in a small container. They must be from the same colony so that they will form a community instead of fight each other.

o Place a glass bowl or jar upside down in the center of the fishbowl. The small jar takes up space in the middle so that the ants will build tunnels and lay eggs close to the sides of the fishbowl, allowing you to see them better.

o Mix together the sand and loose. Fill up the space between the overturned jar and the sides of the fishbowl with the soil-sand mixture. Do not pack down the soil-sand mixture so that the ants can dig easily.

o Dissolve a small amount of sugar and water and place several drops on the sand-soil mixture.

o Place the ants in the fishbowl, being careful that no escape. Cover the fishbowl with the cheesecloth and secure with a rubber band. This will prevent the ants from escaping into places where they are not welcome.

o Cover the outside of the fishbowl with the black construction paper by taping the paper to the fishbowl. This blocks the light so that the ants think that they are underground.

o Place your "ant farm" in a quite area that it will not be disturbed.

Once each day, remove the cheesecloth and add a few drops of sugar water to the soil. Once a week, feed the ants some breadcrumbs.

o After a few days, the ants will begin to build a nest, dig tunnels and compartments, and lay eggs in the sandy soil. Remove the black construction every few days for a short time to observe the ant farm.

• **What you have learned**: Use complete sentences to answer the following questions:

o Can you tell the stages of the life cycle of an ant?

o Describe the stages you observe.


## 4. Growing a Bean Plant

• **What you need:** uncooked, dried lima bean; potting soil; a cup or pot; water; a sunny spot near a window (or outside if the temperature is consistently more than 60 degrees during the day)

• **What you do:**

o The day before you plant the seed, soak it over night in water.

o Fill the cup or pot about ¾ full with potting soil. Push your finger into the soil to make a hole about ½ inch deep. Drop in the seed and cover gently with soil. Add a few drops of water (do not drown the soil).

o Each day, add a few drops of water to the soil. You can also remove the bean from the soil to see if it germinating. Once it sprouts, do not remove it.

o Observe the bean plant go through its life cycle stages: germination, seedling (growth), reproduction, etc.

• **What you have learned**: Use complete sentences to answer the following questions:

o Why did the plants make pods (new seeds) without being pollinated by bees?

o How long did it take your bean to go from seed to mature plant? Could this process be sped up?

## 5. An "Egg-amination": What Are the Parts of an Egg?

• **What you need:** a raw chicken egg; a dish; paper towels; paper and pencil

• **What you do:**

o Hold the raw egg in the palm of your hand and close your fingers around the egg. Squeeze the egg, slowly increasing the pressure until you are squeezing firmly. Do NOT punch your finger through the shell. Observe and record how strong the shell is (how much force the egg can withstand).

o Shake the egg gently back and forth in your hand. Observe and record

the movement inside the egg.

o Gently crack the egg and empty the contents into the dish. Place the egg shell on the paper towel.

o Examine both structure and the texture of the shell. Look in the fat, blunt end of the shell. Can you find a membrane and a space of air?

o Now, examine the contents of the egg.

- Locate the yolk (the yellow part). The yolk would be used by the embryo for energy during development. Notice how the yolk looks like a slightly flattened sphere. If this egg had been fertilized (which the ones we eat are not), the baby bird would develop from the yolk and be attached to it until it hatches.
- Find the small white spot on the top of the yolk. This is where fertilization and the development of the embryo occur.
- Look at the eggs whites. This clear fluid would be used by the developing embryo to help it growth.

o When you're done examining the egg, throw it in the trash and wash your hands.

• **What you have learned**: Use complete sentences to answer the following questions:

o Where does fertilization take place in an egg?

o Which part of the egg will the embryo use for energy?

o Which part of the egg will the embryo use for growth?

# Chapter 7 Quiz

**I. Use each of the following vocabulary words to make each statement correct:**

| fetus | fertilization | metamorphosis | adult | courtship | larva | dormant |
|-------|---------------|---------------|-------|-----------|-------|---------|

1. The process of a male and female bird finding a mate so they can reproduce is called
_____.

2. Some animals like amphibians and insects go through a complete change from egg to adult called a _____.

3. The stages in the life cycle of many insects such as the bee are **egg, _____, pupa** and **adult.**

4. An _____ is the term for a full-grown, mature animal or plant.

5. A seed is _____, which means it is resting, waiting for the right conditions to sprout.

6. _____ occurs when a female and male of a species get together and mix the sperm and an egg.

7. A developing baby inside a mother's uterus is called a _____.

**II. List the stages in each organism's life cycle.**

8. **Bee:** _____, _____, _____, _____

9. **Human**: _____, _____, _____,

_____, _____

10. **Frog:** _____, _____, _____

11. **Bird:** _____, _____, _____,

_____, _____

**III. True or False: Answer each of the following questions by writing a T for true or F for false.**

12. Adolescents are mature and fully-grown. ____

13. Germination is the birth of a plant. ____

14. Only animal organisms have life cycles. ____

15. Pollination is the process of pollen being transferred from the anther of to the stigma. ____

16. Only the queen bee lays eggs. ____

17. A seed is not a living thing. ____

18. Plants have male and female flowers. ____

19. A fledgling is a young bird that is ready to fly away and leave the nest. ____


20. Birds go through a metamorphosis. ____

# Chapter 8: Weather

You know the different types of weather, rainy, cloudy, snowy, and sunny. And you probably also know that weather is different at different places on Earth and that the weather changes in the same location from day-to-day and season-to-season. But, did you ever stop to think what **creates** different types of weather? Before reading further, write a hypothesis of what causes the weather on Earth.

_____

_____

## What Causes Weather?

Weather is a natural occurrence formed by the Earth's **atmosphere**. The atmosphere is a layer of gases that surrounds the Earth. The gases in the atmosphere are commonly referred to as **air**. It acts like a blanket and provides insulation. Without the atmosphere, the heat energy from the sun would escape and Earth would be very cold.

Weather is created because of **pressure** and **temperature** differences. The sun provides the energy that creates all of Earth's weather. The sun does not heat the atmosphere equally. Some air is a cooler temperature and some air is a warmer temperature. These masses of warm and cold air move from place to place. What causes these masses of warm and cold air to move?

Well, cool air is heavier than warm air. That means warm air is lighter and rises while cool air is heavier and sinks. A lot of warm air creates an area of **low pressure**. A lot of cool area creates an area of **high pressure**. Pressure is a force that pushes on molecules (like when someone squeezes your arm hard). The air wants to move from the area of high pressure the area of low pressure. This causes the cool air to sink toward the surface of the Earth to fill up the space left by the rising warm air. Then, the cooler air begins to heat up and rises. This rotation or cycle of cool air and warm air causes **wind**. The greater the difference in temperature between the areas of high and low pressure, the faster the wind blows.

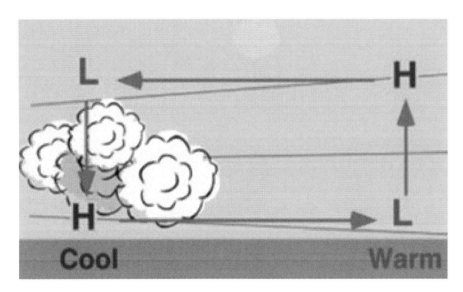

So, the unequal heating of the Earth's atmosphere is the main cause of weather. Stop and compare this reason to your hypothesis.

The main cause for this the unequal heating of the Earth's atmosphere is **latitude** (the measurement of the distance of a location on the Earth starting from the equator). The equator is the hottest part of the Earth. The farther a location is from the equator, the cooler the temperature. That is because the equator receives the most sunlight. The farther from the equator a location is, less sunlight that the location receives. That's why the poles are always cold.

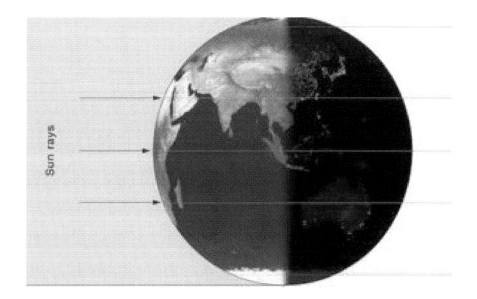

Because of the temperature variations between the equator and the poles, there is always an area of low pressure at the poles (where the air is always cold) and there is always an area higher pressure at the equator (where the air is hot). These two major areas of air pressure on Earth keep the wind constantly moving about or circulating. The winds are then affected by the spin of the Earth. This is called the **Coriolis Effect**.

## Types of Weather

# Precipitation:

When water in any form falls from clouds it is called **precipitation**. Rain is only one form of precipitation. **Snow, sleet** (freezing rain), or **hail** (pea-shaped or larger ice pellets) are other types of precipitation.

The **water cycle** is what creates precipitation. The water cycle begins with **evaporation**. This is when the sun heats up water on the Earth's surface causing the water molecules to evaporate into vapor into the atmosphere. The water molecules begin to group or stick together in a process called **condensation,** and clouds form. The water molecules in clouds eventually become larger and heavier, and gravity pulls them back to the ground in the form of rain.

However, sometimes the temperature of the air and the cloud is below freezing (less than 32°F), so the water molecules form into small ice crystals called snowflakes. Sometime, the clouds are warmer than the air below, and the rain freezes before it hits the ground. This freezing rain is called **sleet**. In other instances, usually during thunderstorms the precipitation gets blown several times back up into the cold atmosphere where it freezes into a small pea-sized ball. This is called **hail**. In larger storms, like the ones that cause tornadoes, the hail can become as large as a softball because of the increased size of the updraft.

## Clouds:

Clouds are caused from **condensation**. The water vapors that form a cloud are so small and so light that they can float in the atmosphere. A cloud is made of billions of water molecules.

Have you ever noticed that not all clouds are the same? There are three main types of clouds: **cumulus, cirrus**, and **stratus**. Then there a unique cloud formation called **fog**. Each one is related to a certain type of weather.

- **Cumulus**: Cumulus clouds are big, puffy, white clouds. These are the ones that look like floating cotton. You may have had fun finding shapes they make. Sometimes, due to changes in pressure and temperature, they can become **cumulonimbus** clouds. These are tall towering cumulus clouds also known as thunderstorm clouds.

- **Cirrus**: Cirrus clouds are high, wispy thin clouds. They are the highest clouds of all. Because the temperature at higher elevations is very cold, cirrus clouds are usually made of ice crystals. Cirrus clouds are a good indicator that more pleasant weather is on the way.

- **Stratus**: The low, flat, grey clouds that cover the entire sky are called stratus. These are the clouds of a day when the weather is "overcast" and can drop cause light rain called drizzle.

- **Fog**: Fog is a low laying cloud that forms at the surface of the Earth.

Which types of clouds do you typically get where you live? _____

_____

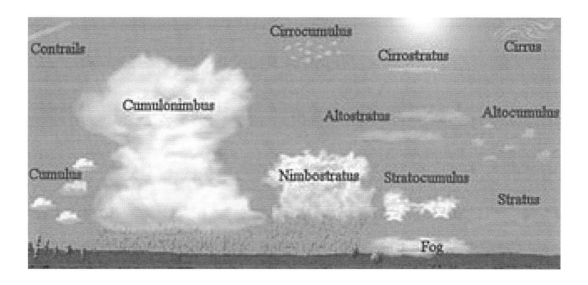

# Weather Fronts:

A **weather front** is a when a warm air mass and a cold air mass meet. This meeting of warm and cold air typically creates some type of stormy weather. There are both **cold fronts** and **warm fronts.**

A **cold front** is when advancing (moving) cold air meets warm air. Remember, cool air is heavier than warm air, so the lighter, warmer air rises while the heavier, cool air sinks At a cold front, the cold air moves rapidly under the warm air, forcing the warmer air to quickly rise. Because the warm air rises so quickly, cold fronts can cause cumulonimbus clouds to form. That brings heavy rain, gusty winds and thunderstorms.

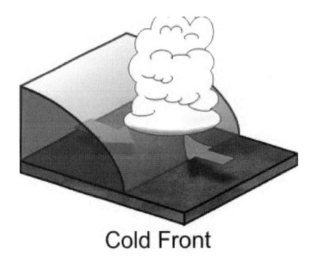

## Cold Front

Does the blue arrow represent warm or cool air? _____
Does the green arrow represent warm or cool air? _____

A **warm front** is when advancing warm air meets cold air. In a warm front, the warm air rises slowly over the top of the cold air. This often traps the lower, cooler clouds causing long periods of light rain or drizzle.

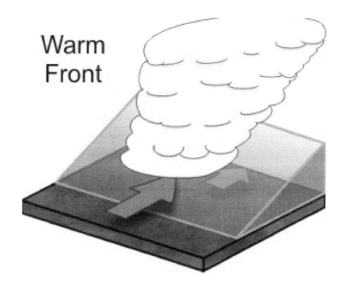

Warm Front

Sometimes a cold front can meet up with a warm front. When this happens it creates what is called an **occluded front**. Occluded fronts can generate heavy rain and thunderstorms, and in extreme cases, tornadoes.

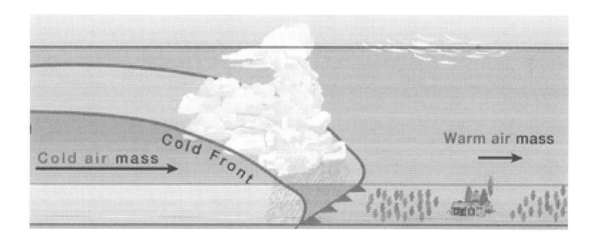

**Thunderstorms:**

A **thunderstorm** is a storm that produces lightning and thunder. They are causes when cumulonimbus cloud form due to changes in pressure and temperature. Thunderstorms typically produce gusty winds, heavy rain, lightning, thunder, and sometimes hail.

Thunderstorms can occur year-round if the conditions are right, but they are most likely to occur in the spring and summer months during the afternoon and evening.

**Lightning** is a discharge of static electricity. Static electricity is nature's way of making opposites attract. That is because positively charged particles are attracted to negatively charged particles. Inside the cloud, water molecules rub together and separate into positive and negative charges. The lightweight positive ice particles gather at the top of the cloud while the heavier negative water particles settle at the bottom. The buildup of negative particles at the bottom of the cloud becomes so great that the charge jumps to the ground where particles are positively charged. This jump emits a giant spark or lightning bolt.

**Thunder** is the noise caused by lightning. Lightning is extremely hot, and the intense heat from lightning causes the surrounding air to rapidly expand. This rapid expansion creates a sonic wave that we hear as thunder. Thunder can sound like a loud crack or a dull rumble. Because light travels faster than sound, we always see lightning before we hear thunder. The closer you are to the lightning, the shorter the gap between the lightning and thunder. Thunder can be heard up to twelve miles away!

Thunderstorms are dangerous and it is good practice to get inside and stay inside during a thunderstorm. There are many reasons to stay safe indoors during a thunderstorm. Lightning strikes can be fatal. There is also the risk of flash flooding which is also responsible for fatalities. Also, there is the potential of tornadoes forming during a thunderstorm, depending on the region in which you live, that can cause a great deal of damage as well as cause fatalities.

# Climate

**Climate** is the temperature and type of weather of a region or area over the course of years. Climate is similar to the weather, but climate is determined by the **average temperature** and **typical weather** patterns over a long period of time. Climate is divided into five types: **tropical, dry, mild, cold,** and **polar**. There are then subcategories, which are **rainforest, desert, tundra, savanna,** and **steppe**.  For example, the climate of most the southwestern United States (like Arizona, Nevada, and New Mexico) is a dry desert. That does not mean that those states don't have rainy or cold days. Just on average, the typical weather is hot and dry.

What is the climate where you live? _____

# Experiments with Weather

Now that you better understand what causes weather and the various types of weather, it's time to put that knowledge to use and conduct some experiments related to weather.

## 1. What causes precipitation in the form of rain?

**Research:** Briefly research or think about what you already know about how precipitation and rain are formed.

**Hypothesis:** Write your own educated guess as a statement that answers the question.
**Materials:** a glass jar; a plate; very hot water; ice cubes; index cards

**Procedure:**
o With the help of an adult, bring to a slow boil enough water to fill the glass jar 2 inches full. Carefully pour the very hot water into the glass jar so that water is about 2 inches deep.

o Cover the jar with the plate. Let the plate rest on the jar for two minutes.

o Add enough ice cubes to cover the plate.

o Observe and record what occurs inside the jar for at least 10 minutes.

**Observations:** Describe what happened inside the jar.

**Conclusion:**

o Was your hypothesis correct? How did rain appear inside the jar?

## 2. What causes condensation or clouds to form?

**Research:** Briefly research or think about what you already know about how condensation and clouds form.

**Hypothesis:** Write your own educated guess as a statement that answers the question.
**Materials:** 1-liter clear plastic bottle with cap; a foot pump; rubber stopper (the size of the opening to the bottle); rubber tubing; water; rubbing alcohol; safety glasses

**Procedure:**

o Put on the safety glasses. This important because you will be pressurizing the bottle and the stopper could pop off.

o Pour just enough warm water into the bottle to just cover the bottom.

Then, swirl the water around.

o Attach the rubber stopper to the tube of the foot pump and then put the rubber stopper into the bottle to replace the cap.

o Pump the foot pump five times. As you start to pump, you'll notice the rubber stopper will want to pop out. Hold the stopper tightly against the bottle so it will not pop out.

o After five successful pumps, pull the stopper out of the bottle. You should see a very faint cloud. Now you will attempt to make a more visible cloud.

o Fill the bottle with just enough water to cover the bottom and swirl. Repeat the steps above, this time attempting to get ten pumps into the bottle. Hold the stopper tightly to the bottle. When you have ten successful pumps, pull out the stopper. This time you should see a slightly more visible cloud.

o Add a bit more water to replace what escaped and repeat the steps above, but pump the foot pump 15-20 times. Remove the rubber stopper. You should see an even more visible cloud.

o Once you mastered the steps above (and have successful gotten 15 pumps of air into the bottle), place just a few drops of rubbing alcohol in the bottom of bottle. Swirl the alcohol around in the bottle so that sides are well coated. Put the rubber stopper in the bottle. Hold the stopper firmly and try to pump 15 times. Remove the stopper to see a very visible cloud.

**Observations:** Describe what happened as you added more air pressure and when you used rubbing alcohol instead of water.

**Conclusion:**

o Was your hypothesis correct? How did a cloud appear inside the jar? Why do you think rubbing alcohol was used instead of just water? How did increasing the air pressure form a cloud?

## 3. What causes wind?

**Research:** Briefly research or think about what you already know wind.

**Hypothesis:** Write your own educated guess as a statement that answers the question.
**Materials:** two (2) metal baking pans; two heat resistant pads or wood boards; and oven; an oven mitt; a large cardboard box; clean, dry sand; ice; one (1) incense stick; scissors; matches

## Procedure:
o Fill the first baking pan with sand and place in an oven on the lowest heat setting.

o Using the scissors, cut off the front of the cardboard box.

o Place the heat resistant pads or (wooden board) inside the box. The pads or boards need to be big enough to hold the two baking pans.

o Fill the second baking pan with ice and place it on one of the pads inside the box.

o After about 10 minutes, using the oven mitt remove the baking pan with sand from the over. Place it in the box on the pad so that the two baking pans are touching.

o Take a match and light an incense stick. Hold it horizontally with the burning tip right between the two pans.

**Observations:** Describe what happened to the smoke from the incense stick (the smoke will always drift toward the warm baking pan full of sand).
## Conclusion:

o Was your hypothesis correct? Why did the smoke drift towards the warm baking pan full of sand?

o How do you know? What evidence supports your conclusion?


## 4. How can we tell how fast the wind is blowing?

**Research:** Briefly research or think about what you already know about how wind speed is calculated. Find out what an anemometer is.

**Hypothesis:** Write your own educated guess as a statement that answers the question.
**Materials:** 5 paper cups: a wooden skewer; 2 straws; a pencil with an eraser scissors; a push pin; a permanent marker; tape

**Procedure:**

o Take four of the cups and punch one hole in each using the wood skewer, about ½ inch below the rim. Take the last cup and punch two holes in it, directly opposite from each other, about ½ inch below the rim. Last, poke two more holes in the 5th cup, each ¼ inch below the rim and equally-spaced between the first two holes.

o Use the push-pin and the scissors to make a hole in the center of the bottom of the 5th cup (the one with four holes in it). The hole should be just wide enough that the pencil can fit through it easily.

| Revolutions in 10 sec. | Wind speed in mph |
|---|---|
| 2-4 | 1 |
| 5-7 | 2 |
| 8-9 | 3 |
| 10-12 | 4 |

o Slide one of the straws through the hole in one of the four cups with only one hole in it. Bend the end of the straw s inside the cup about ½ and tape it flat to the inside of the cup. Place the other end of the straw through the two holes in the5th cup and then through the hole in one of the other cups. Tape the end of the straw to the inside of the cup as before, making sure that the openings of the two cups face opposite directions.

o Repeat steps with the remaining two cups, sliding the straw through the two remaining holes in the 5th cup. Make sure that the opening of each cup faces the bottom of the cup next to it and each of the four cups are facing sideways.

o Insert the pencil with the eraser facing up through the bottom of the 5th cup. Then, push the pin through the two straws and into the eraser.

o Take the permanent marker and draw a large X on the bottom of only one of the cups.

| 13-15 | 5 |
|-------|----|
| 16-18 | 6 |
| 19-21 | 7 |
| 22-23 | 8 |
| 24-26 | 9 |
| 27-29 | 10 |

**Observations:** Describe what happened to the anemometer the harder the wind blew.

**Conclusion:**

o Was your hypothesis correct?

o How do you know? What evidence supports your conclusion?

## 5. How can we tell if weather will change?

**Research:** Briefly research or think about what you already know about how changes in pressure. Find out what a barometer is.

**Hypothesis:** Write your own educated guess as a statement that answers the question.
**Materials:** a balloon; scissors; a jar; a rubber band; tape; a straw; an index card; a marker or pen

**Procedure:**

o Cut off the end of the balloon that you blow into and stretch the opening of the balloon over the mouth of the jar. About half of the balloon should flop over the side of the jar. Hold the balloon in place by stretching the rubber band over the balloon at the rim of the jar.

o Place the straw horizontally at the top of the jar so that about 1/3 of the straw is hanging over the edge. This will be the pointer of the barometer. Attach the straw to the balloon with tape.

o Draw three lines at the center of the index card about half a centimeter apart. Label these lines high, moderate and low.

o Tape the card against he jar so that the straw points to moderate.

o Put the barometer on a flat surface somewhere inside (not outdoors).

o When there is low air pressure the balloon should expand and the straw will point down. That is because the air inside the balloon and jar now has relatively more air pressure compared to the air outside, so it causes the balloon to expand.

o When there is high air pressure the air on the outside of the balloon and jar will push the balloon into the jar and the straw will point upwards. The air inside the balloon now has relatively less pressure and this pushes the balloon into the jar.

**Observations:** Describe what happened to the barometer and compare it to the weather each day. Usually, high air pressure indicates nice is likely weather while low air pressure indicates that bad weather is likely.

**Conclusion:**

o Was your hypothesis correct?

o How do you know? What evidence supports your conclusion?

# Chapter 8 Quiz

**I. Use each of the following vocabulary words to make each statement correct:**

| climate   atmosphere   warm front   cold front   thunder   Coriolis Effect |
|---|

1. The noise cause by a sonic wave because of lightning is called _____.

2. Long periods of light rain or drizzle is often caused by a _____ _____.

3. Winds caused temperature variations between the equator and the poles and the spin of the Earth cause the _____.

4. _____ is the temperature and type of weather of a region or area over the course of years.

5. The unequal heating of the Earth's _____ is the main cause of weather.

6. A _____ _____ produces heavy rains, gusty winds and possible thunderstorms.

**II. Circle the word that correctly completes each statement.**

7. Clouds that form at the surface of the Earth are called (cirrus) (fog).

8. During a thunderstorm is it safest to be (indoors) (outdoors).

9. Thunderstorms are cause by cumulonimbus clouds and produce gusty winds, (heavy

rains) (drizzle), and sometimes thunder, lightning and hail.

10. The rotation or cycle of cool air and warm air causes (fog) (wind).

11. (Precipitation) (Condensation) is the part of the water cycle in which clouds are formed.

12. (Stratus) (cirrus) clouds are the highest clouds, are very cold, and are usually made of ice crystals.

13. Tornadoes can sometime occur when at cold front catches up to a warm front, which is called an (occasional front) (occluded front).

14. Rain, snow, sleet and hail are all types of (precipitation) (evaporation).

15. Warm air is lighter than cool air, and so warm air (rises) (sinks).

16. The low, flat, grey clouds that cover the entire sky and cause drizzle are called (stratus) (cumulus).

17. The sun heats the atmosphere (equally) (unequally) and this causes differences in temperature and pressure that creates weather.


**III. Think like a scientist. Answer each question in several complete sentences.**


18. What is the difference between weather and climate?
19. What are weather fronts and what do they cause?
20. What are the differences between cloud types?

# Chapter 9: Earth and How It Changes

## Our Home: The Earth

Your house is your home, but did you know we call many places our home? That's because a home is any place you live and on Earth that includes a variety of places. You live in your house that is in a town or city. That city is part of a country and each country is on a **continent**. There are seven **continents** or landmasses on Earth: Asia, Africa, North America, South America, Europe, Australia, and Antarctica.

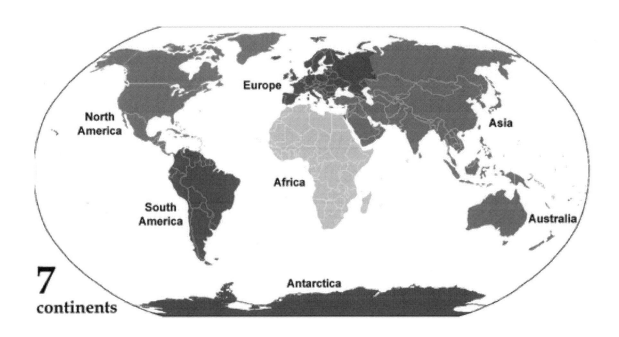

Earth is our home planet. But what is a planet?

A planet is a **sphere** (a ball) that is large enough to have its own **gravity** (the force that holds everything to a planet's surface). A planet also revolves around a sun. Earth is one of the eight planets in the Solar System that all go around the sun.

The Earth is the third planet from the sun. It's not too warm or too cold, making it perfect for the existence and survival of living things. Plants, animals and people all share the Earth on which we live. Scientists who study the Earth and how it changes are called **geologist**. Get ready to study more about Earth's geology!

## Composition: What is the Earth Made of?

The Earth is primarily an enormous ball of **rock**. The Earth is composed of four layers, a bit like a hardboiled egg. The layers are the **crust** (like the shell), the **mantle** (like the egg white), the **outer core** and the **inner core** (like the yolk).

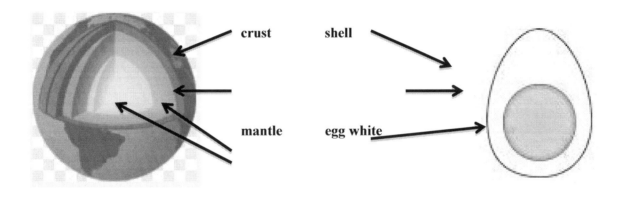

The surface of the Earth is covered with land (rocks and soil), water and a huge variety of organisms (living things). About 30% of the surface is land that scientists call **landmasses.** Landmasses are just as the name implies, large masses of land. The other 70% of the surface is covered with water (oceans, rivers, ponds, etc.). Underneath the water, land, plants, animals and other organism is the **crust** of the Earth. The crust of the Earth varies in thickness between 3 miles on the ocean floor and around 40 miles at the tallest point of the land.  The crust is composed of rock. Geologists categorize all rocks into three types: **igneous, metamorphic,** and **sedimentary.** Every rock is composed of **elements**. There are 90 known elements that exist in the Earth's crust. Natural processes combine these 90 elements in a number ways that create what are known as **minerals.**

With so many possible combinations, there must be a whole lot of minerals. Well, indeed! There are around 3,700 known minerals and new minerals are being discovered every year!

The **mantle** is much thicker and harder than the crust. It extends to a depth of around 1,800 miles. Because the mantel is so dense (the molecules are packed very closely together) it accounts for around 85% of the total mass of the Earth.

Below the mantle lies the **outer core**, which extends to a depth of around 3000 mile. Because humans cannot travel or drill below the surface to such great depths, geologist must hypothesis about its composition by studying seismic waves caused by earthquakes as well as information provided from studying volcanoes. Geologists believe that the outer core is composed of extremely hot liquid or molten lava that is mostly likely mostly made of iron and nickel.

The **inner core** is the center of the earth. Geologists believe that the inner core is a solid ball composed of mostly iron and nickel. Again, very little is known about the inner core because of its great depth below the Earth's surface.

## How Earth Changes

The Earth changes constantly. These changes have both terrified and fascinated people for a long time. Some changes happen right before your eyes, like **earthquakes, mudslides, floods, avalanches** and **volcanic eruptions**. These geological changes are violent and can cause serious harm to people and animals. They change the environment dramatically when they occur.

The Earth's crust is not one solid piece of rock like the shell of an egg. Rather, it is broken up into huge, thick pieces called **plates** that drift on top of the softer, liquid mantle. These plates range from 50 to 250 miles in thickness. The plates drift all over the surface of the Earth. This is called **continental drift**. Continental drift is one way the Earth changes. Over millions of years, the plates have changed in size and shape as they have shifted, been crushed together, and pushed back down into the mantle. The plates move between 1 and 10 centimeters each year. The result of the plates moving, drifting and crushing is **seismic activity** also known as **earthquakes** and **volcanoes**. Scientists refer to the movements plates make as **plate tectonics**.

Where the plates meet a variety of slipping and buckling occurs that causes seismic activity. If two plates collide, a **mountain range** is formed. When one plate is pushed under another, magma can be pushed out from the mantle, forming a **volcano**. Two plates can also move sideways against each other. Eventually the plates slip, and if pressure is released suddenly, the plates will jerk apart. This is how an **earthquake** occurs. The plates also separate from one another. This is called seafloor spreading and magma forms new oceanic crust. The movement of the continental plates resulting in earthquakes and volcanoes can cause a great deal of destruction to the environment. It can be devastating to the cities and to the people in the vicinity of the seismic activity.

Other geological changes occur on Earth that is not related to plate tectonics. **Weathering, erosion** and **deposition** are three ways that the Earth changes more slowly. **Weathering** is the process where rock is broken down or worn away through various types of weather like wind and rain. Weathering changes large chunks of rock into smaller and smaller piece such as pebble and sand. Smaller pieces of rock are called **sediment**. Weathering can even dissolve some of the minerals in certain types of rocks. For example, the constant dripping of water through limestone causes caves to form. One of the most impressive forms of weathering is the movement of sand in the desert that creates the constantly changing shape of sand dunes.

Once weathering has broken down rock, it can be moved, changing the landscape of the Earth, in a process called **erosion.** Erosion occurs when rocks and sediments are picked up and moved by ice, water, wind or gravity. Once erosion has stopped moving sediment, it piles up or gets deposited. The depositing of sediments due to erosion is called **deposition**. Let's look at a few geological changes due to weather, erosion and deposition.

**Glaciers** are slow moving, masses of ice that can carve (erode) valleys and deposit huge piles of rock and sediment.

**Rivers** can cut (erode) valleys and form deltas. A **delta** is a landform that is created at the mouth a river from deposits of sediment (rock and soil) carried by the river. The image below is not a leaf or a tree. It is a delta, the deposition of sediment at the mouth of a river.

A **coast** if formed by waves and tides eroding shorelines and building beaches where the ocean meets the land. The constant movement of the water breaks apart or weathers rocks turning them first into pebbles and eventually into sand.

Can you think of other ways the Earth goes through geological changes?

_____

There are other changes that happen much more slowly, over thousands even millions of years. A change of the Earth that can take millions of years to happen is called **the rock cycle**. The rock cycle is a process of the Earth changing rocks from igneous to metamorphic to sedimentary and back to igneous. A rock cycle is different from a life cycle that plants and animals go through. That is because rocks may change back and for between different parts of the cycle in practically any order.

Here one basic way the rock cycle works:

1. Molten (liquid) rock called magma reaches the earth's surface during volcanic activity. When magma reaches the surface and hits air or water, it cools and forms into an **igneous**

rock.

2. Weather and water slowly break up the igneous rock into small pieces of sediment.

3. As sediment builds up, it begins to harden over many, many years. Layers of sediment form **sedimentary** rock. Sometimes plants and animals get buried in these layers and a fossil forms.

4. Over thousands and thousands of years, this sedimentary rock gets covered with other rocks and end up deep in the Earth's crust where heat and pressure causes rock to undergo a metamorphosis and change once again into **metamorphic** rock.

5. If enough pressure and heat occurs, metamorphic rock can become magma, and the cycle will start over again.

The diagram below shows many of the variations of the rock cycle.

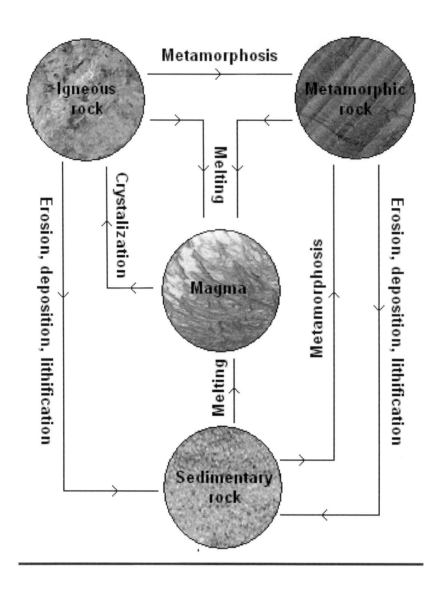

## Soil

Geologist can study the surface of the Earth very thoroughly. One very important component of the surface is the land. Land is made of rocks and **soil**. Soil is commonly referred to as dirt.

Soil is composed of a mixture of many things. It's made up of minerals, water, air, organic material (dead plants and animals), and millions bacteria. Soil is a process of the changing Earth. That is why soil is also sometimes called earth (with a lower case "e").

Yes, the Earth makes earth. It is formed at the surface and is vital to supporting plants, which in turn allow for animals to exist on Earth. Soil is an important part of all ecosystems (deserts, forests, tundra, grasslands, etc.). Soil provides many things crucial for an ecosystem. Soil provides:

- plants a place to grow
- the nutrients plants need for growth
- a habitat for mammals (such as groundhogs and mice) and other organisms like bacteria and fungi that live in soil

List 4 animals that live in the soil:

_____, _____, _____, _____,

Soil also recycles nutrients so that living things can use them over and over again. It also acts like a filter, cleaning water before it moves back into the water cycle.

# Experiments with The Earth and How It Changes

Now that your knowledge on the topic of geology has been expanded, let's to use what you have learned. The following experiments will help you become an even more knowledgeable geologist.

## 1. How do rocks change in the rock cycle?

**Research:** Briefly research or think about what you already know about the rock cycle and how igneous, metamorphic and sedimentary rocks are formed.

**Hypothesis:** Write your own educated guess as a statement that answers the question.
**Materials:** several blocks of dark and white chocolate; aluminum foil (or aluminum foil cupcake holders); a pot; a stove; water; measure cups; plastic knife; paper and pencil

**Procedure:**
o Begin by making "sedimentary" rock. Using the knife, scrape ¼ cup small shavings from the block of chocolate.

o Collect the scrapings and put them in pile into a piece of aluminum foil. Wrap the shavings with the aluminum foil and then press down with all your body weight. Next, put it on the ground and stand on enclosed foil package.

o On a table or counter, unwrap the foil. Observe and record the sedimentary "rock": observe and record what happened to the chocolate scrapings in the foil after apply pressure.

o Next, make "metamorphic" rock. Take a new piece of foil and shape it into a small canoe or rowboat. Place the "sedimentary rock", about 1 tablespoon of white chocolate shavings, and two or three small chunks of the white chocolate block (break off a few small pieces with by hand) into the aluminum foil boat. This time, you will not use pressure to squeeze the pieces together.

o With the help of an adult, heat water in the pot, just before boiling. Now, place the aluminum foil boat and its contents onto the surface of the water so that it floats.

o Observe and record how the heat from the water transfers to the foil and the chocolate (the chocolate should start to melt and the white and brown colors blend slightly).

o Carefully remove the foil boat with the plastic knife when the chocolate is soft to the touch. Allow the chocolate to cool and harden into a "metamorphic rock". Observe and record the cooled "metamorphic rock".

o Last, make an "igneous rock". Place the " metamorphic rock" and some small chunks from both blocks of chocolate into a piece aluminum foil, again shaping the foil into a boat.

o With the help of an adult, bring water to a boil. Remove the pot from the heat and float the foil with its contents on the surface of the very hot water.

o Observe and record how the heat transfers from the water to the foil, melting chocolate. Allow the chocolate to melt into a smooth liquid or "magma".

o Carefully remove the "magma" (molten chocolate) with the knife. Pour the magma onto a flat sheet of aluminum foil.

o Observe and record how the lava flows then cools and hardens into "igneous rock".

o When you are finished, eat your rock cycle chocolate if you chose.

**Observations:** Describe what happened during each stage of the rock cycle.

**Conclusion:**

o Was your hypothesis correct?

o How do you know? What evidence supports your conclusion?

o How did this experiment model the rock cycle?

**2. How do fossils form?**

**Research:** Briefly research or think about what you already know about fossils and how they form in the layering process of sedimentary rocks.

**Hypothesis:** Write your own educated guess as a statement that answers the question.
**Materials:** paper towels; one slice of white bread; one slice of wheat bread; one slice of rye bread; three (3) gummy candy fish or worms; several heavy books; a hand lens; clear plastic straws

**Procedure:**

o Place one paper towel on a flat surface. Carefully remove the crust from each piece of bread.

o Place the piece of white bread  paper towel. This represents the ocean floor. Put one gummy on the bread.

o Place the piece of rye bread on top of the white bread and gummy. This layer shows deposition of sediments on top of a dead organism.

o Add the remaining gummy candy, and then the slice of wheat bread. This represents the deposition of additional sediments due to weathering and erosion.

o Fold the paper towel over the top of the layers of bread and gummies. Add pressure by placing several heavy books on top of the "sedimentary rock" (bread and gummies).

o Leave the books on top for two days (about 48 hours) to represent the millions of years it takes for a fossil to form within sedimentary rock.

o After two days, unwrap the "sedimentary rock". Push a clear straw straight down into and through the layers of bread and pull it back up to "extract" a core sample. Observe and record the layers in the straw.

o Now, try to separate the layers of the bread. You will notice that it is difficult to do so.

o Finally, pull out a gummy. Observe and record the gummy "fossil's" impression in the bread and any residue from the gummy that seeped into the bread.

**Observations:** Describe the core sample, the layers after they were under pressure and the impression left by the gummy.

**Conclusion:**

o Was your hypothesis correct?

o How do you know? What evidence supports your conclusion?

o How did this model the formation of fossils? How was it different?


**3. How does a glacier erode the land and deposit sediment?**

**Research:** Briefly research or think about what you already know glacier and how they erode the land and deposit sediment.

**Hypothesis:** Write your own educated guess as a statement that answers the question.
**Materials:** one (1) half-gallon milk carton, 12' x 1' panel or board; sand; small rocks; gravel (considerable smaller than the rocks); a freezer; a warm day (between 60°F and 80 °F); scissors; paper and pencil

## Procedure:

o Use the scissors to remove one side from the milk carton.

o Fill carton one-third full with a mixture of sand, rocks and gravel and water. Place the container and its contents in a freezer.

o Remove the carton once the mixture has frozen solid and fill the container another one-thirds full with a mixture of sand, rocks and gravel and water. Place the container back in the freezer.

o When the mixture is frozen again, fill the carton completely with a mixture of sand, rock, gravel and water. Freeze once more until solid.

o When the outdoor temperature is above 60°F and below 80°F, lay out the board or panel at approximately a 20° angle.

o At the top of the panel, spread some gravel about 1 inch thick. Remove the frozen block from the carton and place it at the top of the panel behind the gravel.

o Record and observe movement of the block gravel for at least 1 hour.

**Observations:** Describe what happened to the block as it melted. Describe the formations created.
## Conclusion:

o Was your hypothesis correct?

o How do you know? What evidence supports your conclusion?


## 4. How does an earthquake?

**Research:** Briefly research or think about what you already know about how earthquakes occur when two plates slip.

**Hypothesis:** Write your own educated guess as a statement that answers the question.
**Materials:** a square (about 8 x 8) baking pan; two packages of Jell-O (any color); a

spoon; a measuring cup; plastic wrap; a knife; a spoon; a pot; a stove

**Procedure:**

o With the help of an adult, follow the direction on the Jell-O box. Measure and pour the indicated amount of water for two packages of Jell-O into the pot, and heat it to a rolling boil.

o Carefully pour the boiling water into the baking pan. Stir in the powdered gelatin using the spoon.

o Place the pan into the refrigerator for several hours, making sure it is sitting flat, until the Jell-O is firm.

o Cut two pieces of plastic wrap (each one should be long enough to hold half the Jell-O) and lay the two halves on a flat surface so that the halves are touching each other.

o Remove the pan of Jell-O from the refrigerator. Fill a sink or large container with about 2 inches of warm water. Float the pan in the warm water until the Jell-O can easily be removed.

o Now, gently slide the Jell-O out of the pan and onto the plastic wrap, so that half of the Jell-O on each side piece of the plastic wrap.

o Cut in the Jell-O along the same place as the space between in the plastic wrap.

o Slowly slide the two chunks of Jell-O past each other, pulling the plastic wrap with the Jell-O on top in opposite directions. Each chunk of Jell-O represents a tectonic plate of the Earth.

**Observations:** Describe what happened the chunks of Jell-O when they slid past each other (you will see the Jell-O shift and shake like an earthquake).

**Conclusion:**

o Was your hypothesis correct?

o How do you know? What evidence supports your conclusion?

**5. How does erosion change the landscape and move sediment?**

**Research:** Briefly research or think about what you already know about erosion and deposition.

**Hypothesis:** Write your own educated guess as a statement that answers the question.

**Materials:** a plastic container about the size of a shoe box; a pitcher; sand; soil; Styrofoam cup; a clear plastic cup or bottle; water; masking tape; a paper and pencil

## Procedure:

o Have an adult help you drill or cut a hole (about ½ inch in diameter) in the bottom of the container at the center of one end. Place masking tape over the hole on the outside of the container. You will remove the tape later.

o Pour sand and soil (the soil in your yard works just fine) into the container. With your hands, mix the sand and soil, then level the sand and soil mixture and pat it down lightly

o On a table or desk, elevate the end of the container WITHOUT the hole about 3 to 4 inches by placing it on a block or book. That is so the water you pour in will drain out the hole at the lower end. You are creating a hill for water to run down and erode the sand and soil.

o Slide the tilted container to the end of the table or desk and place the plastic cup or bottle under the container on the ground. If you're doing this inside, place several paper towels under the plastic cup.

o Use the pencil to poke a hole in the Styrofoam cup the width of the pencil. Tape the cup to the elevated end of the container about 2 inches from the sand and soil mixture.

o Fill the water pitcher. Slowly pour a constant stream of water into the cup. Continue to pour water into the cup until the pitcher is empty.

o Once the water begins to reach the bottom of the "hill, remove the tape and adjust the plastic cup or bottle directly under the hole to catch the run-off.

o Observe and record what happens as you poured the water into the cup.

**Observations:** Describe the erosion and deposition that occurred. Describe any "land formations" that were created by the erosion and deposition like a river, pond or delta. Describe the sediment and run-off in the plastic cup or bottle.

## Conclusion:

o Was your hypothesis correct?

o How do you know? What evidence supports your conclusion?

# Chapter 9 Quiz

**I. Use each of the following vocabulary words to make each statement correct:**

| mantle | delta | sedimentary | erosion | rock cycle | rock |
|---|---|---|---|---|---|

1. The crust of the Earth is composed of three types of rocks: igneous, metamorphic and _____.

2. The movement of sediment by water, wind or gravity is called _____.

3. The Earth's layers are the crust, _____, outer core and inner core.

4. An example of deposition at the mouth of a river is called a _____.

5. The Earth is composed primarily of _____.

6. The _____ is a process of the Earth changing rocks from igneous to metamorphic to sedimentary and back to igneous.

**II. Draw a line between each step of the scientific method and its definition.**

7. **Weathering**          Massive, slow moving amounts of ice that can

                           carve valleys and deposit sediment

8. **Igneous**          The depositing of sediments due to erosion

9. **Glacier**                   Process that rock is worn away and broke down

by wind and rain

10. **Deposition**             Dirt or earth

11. **Continents**            A type of rock formed when magma cools and

hardens

11. **Soil**                       The landmasses on the Earth's surface

**III. True or False: Answer each of the following questions by writing a T for true or F for false.**

12. Continental drift is the movement of plates of the crust on top of the mantle. ____

13. Fossils can be found in the layers of sedimentary rock.____

14. Scientists that study the earth and how it changes are called biologists. ____

15. When two plates move sideways against each other they eventually slip. If pressure is released suddenly, the plates will jerk apart causing a volcano. ____

16. Because humans cannot travel or drill below the surface to great depths below the surface of the Earth, geologist must hypothesis about the composition of the inner and

outer core. _____


17. Soil is made of minerals, water, air, organic material (dead plants and animals), but not bacteria. _____


18. Metamorphic rock is formed deep in the Earth's crust where heat and pressure causes rock to undergo a metamorphosis. _____


**IV. Think like a scientist. Answer each question in 1-2 complete sentences.**


19. How is the Earth like a hardboiled egg? *The crust is like the shell of an egg. The mantle is like the egg whites. The inner and outer core are like the yolk.*

20. Why is soil important to the Earth? *Soil allows for plants to grow. It gives plants a place to grow and provides plants nutrients needed to grow. It provides a habitat for animals. It also acts like a filter to clean the water on Earth.*

# Answer Key

## Chapter 1:

1. **Evidence** is what all scientists must use to show or confirm the statements about their investigations are true.

2. **Numerical** data is the use numbers that measure something, such as height, length, time, rate, etc.

3. A changing quantity in the cause and effect of the experiment is called a **variable** and only one at a time should be changed in an experiment.

4. The process that scientists use to study, learn and investigate scientific questions is called the **Scientific Method**.

5. Scientists conduct **experiments** to find out answers to questions.

6. **Question**            The topic or idea the scientist wants to learn about

7. **Research**            Information collected during an experiment

8. **Hypothesis**          An educated guess that answers the question

9. **Procedure**           Step-by-step directions for an experiment

10. **Data**               Gathering of information

11. **Observations**       Written description of what was noticed during

                           an experiment

12. **Conclusion**         A statement telling whether or not

                           the hypothesis was correct

**III. True or False: Answer each of the following questions by writing a T for truc or F for false.**

13. Only adult biologists are considered scientists. (F)

14. A hypothesis must be correct for an experiment to be valid. (F)

15. Science is a continuing process that builds on what was learned before. (T)

16. Observations are keeping records of things that are noticed during an experiment like color, texture, smell, as well as errors, uncontrolled variables and anything surprising or unexpected. (T)

17. When writing the procedures or designing an experiment, it is important to test or manipulate multiple variables at a time. (F)

18. In the Scientific Method the question must be something that can be measured. (T)

19. The procedure is a step-by-step plan or guide is designed which serve as directions which must also list the materials needed. (T)

20. Doing some basic research will help you write a better hypothesis. (T)

# Chapter 2:

**I. Determine if each is a physical or chemical change. Circle the word chemical or physical.**

1. **folding paper**: chemical   physical

2. **breaking a pencil**: chemical   physical

3. **bread molding**: chemical   physical

4. **popcorn kernels popping**: chemical   physical

5. **hydrogen peroxide bubbling on a cut**: chemical   physical

6. **whipping an egg:** chemical   physical

7. **water boiling:** chemical   physical

8. **sanding wood:** chemical   physical

9. **painting a car:** chemical   physical

10. **gas igniting:** chemical  physical

11. What is the "stuff" that all things are made up of, has mass and takes up space? *Matter*

12. What type of change happens at the molecular level? *Chemical*

13. Which type of change is usually reversible? *Physical*

14. Would a physical or chemical change produce a new odor or bubbles? *Chemical*

15. In what phase of matter does a substance take on the shape of the container it is in? *Liquid*

16. When energy is added (increasing the temperature) to a substance such as water, what is the result? *It moves to the next state of matter.*

17. In a physical or chemical change do the atoms rearrange to create a new substance? *Chemical*

18. What is another word for a state of matter? *A phase*


19. How could you tell if physical reaction was taking place? *It could be changed back like water to ice and ice to water or nothing new was created.*

20. What kind of things might occur to tell you a chemical change was occurring and a new substance was being formed? *There could be bubbles, a new smell or taste, heat, or light.*

# Chapter 3:

1. Plasma is the most common type of matter found in the **universe.**

2. Electricity **moves through** matter.

3. **Lightning** is a type of static electricity.

4. **Salt water** is a conductor.

5. **Plasmas** carry an electric current and generate a magnetic field.

6. When enough energy in the form of heat is added to a gas, it becomes **plasma.**

7. Plasma and gases **do not have** definite shape, so the atoms spread out evenly and take on the shape of their container.

8. **Plasma** does not have a neutral charge like the other states of matter because they are both positively charged **(+)** and negatively charged **(-).**

9. Neon signs and florescent light bulbs get very hot. (F)

10. The Northern Lights are caused by plasma due to solar winds. (T)

11. Glass is a conductor and does not conduct electricity. (F)

12. When a gas is ionized sufficient energy is provided to free electrons from atoms or molecules, so both ions and electrons now exist together. (T)

13. Protons carry a negative charge. Electrons carry positive charge. (F)

14. Plasma is not commonly found on Earth in nature. It is more commonly found as man-made materials. (T)

15. Hydrogen and helium are common gases found in neon signs. (F)

16. Electricity is the 4$^{th}$ state of matter. (F)

17. plasma: some possible answers include lightning, the Northern Lights, florescent light bulbs and neon signs

18. static electricity: some possible answer are lightning, rubbing a comb or balloon on hair, walking across a wool carpet

19. conductor: some possible answers include iron, steel and water

20. insulator: some possible answers include rubber, plastic, glass and wood

# Chapter 4:

1. **Mitochondria** are the battery of powerhouse of cells because they provide energy for the cell.

2. Complex organisms that have cells that contain a nucleus are called **eukaryote**.

3. A spiral ladder of DNA that cells use to replicate is called a **double helix**.

4. **Replication** is process of cell division that allows a cell to make more of themselves.

5. **Chloroplast** is the green part of plants.

6. ~~water:~~

7. mold: Organism (circled)

8. insects: Organism (circled)

9. ~~a fire~~

10. ~~wind~~

11. flowers: Organism (circled)

12. ~~the sun~~

13. an uncooked egg: Organism (circled)

14. a seed: Organism (circled)

15. ~~crystals~~

16. bacteria: Organism (circled)

17. mushrooms in the ground (not at the grocery store): Organism (circled)


18. Why are viruses not considered organisms or living things? *Viruses have to have a host to multiply and cannot survive or replicate on their own without a host.*

19. How are plant cells different from animal cells? *They are shaped differently (plant cells are more square shaped and animal cells more circular), but most importantly only plant cells contain chloroplast so they can go through the process of photosynthesis.*

20. What evidence can you use to prove a cat is an organism? *Cats move on their own,*

*need food, water and air to survive, take in energy to grow, reproduce, respond and adapt to their environment.*

# Chapter 5:

1. **visible spectrum**   The wavelengths of light humans can see.

2. **reflection**   When a light hits an object and bounces off.

3. **photons**   Tiny particles of which light is made.

4. **electromagnetic**   The various wavelengths of light.

   **spectrum**

5. **refraction**   The slowing and bending of light as it travels through matter such as air or water.

6. **white light**   Also known as visible light.

7. **prism**   Glass or raindrops that separate white light into its colors.

8. **incandescent lamp**   The simplest type of light bulb containing filament.

9. **florescent lamp**   A light bulb that send electrical discharge through an ionized gas.

10. **sun**   Light that allows life to exist on Earth.


11. Light is energy. (T)

12. Light has mass and an electrical charge. (F)

13. Humans can see all wavelengths of light.( F)

14. ROY G. BIV is an acronym for the order of colors in the visible spectrum. (T)

15. Reflection is the bending of light as it passes through matter. (F)

16. Light moves at the fastest known speed in the universe. (T)

17. Ordinary daylight appears white or colorless. (T)

18. Gamma rays have the largest (farthest apart) wavelength and least amount of energy. (F)

19. What would happen to the Earth if there it no long received light from the sun? *Plants and animals would die from lack of warmth and energy. Life would no longer exist.*

20. What's the difference between reflection and refraction? *Reflection is the bouncing off of light from an object like a mirror or pond. Refraction is the bending of light when it passes through matter such as water or glass.*

# Chapter 6:

1. Name the body system helps humans turn the food they eat into energy (Digestive)

2. Name the body system helps humans breathe (Respiratory)

3. Name the body system controls other body systems (Nervous)

4. Name the body system provides structure for the body. (Skeletal)

5. Name the body system allows us to move. (Muscular)

6. Name the body system transports blood and with a pump (the heart). (Circulatory)

7. What are two body systems that work together? (Possible correct answers include: the respiratory and circulatory, muscular and skeletal, digestive and circulatory, and nervous and any other system.)

8. Which organ of the nervous system is most important for it to work properly? (Brain)

9. What can cause harm to one or more body systems? (Possible correct answers include: germs, sickness, injury or disease could disrupt one or more body systems)

10. Which system is responsible for protecting the body and fighting off germs? (Immune)

11. What are two jobs of the endocrine system? (Possible correct answers include: regulate mood, control growth, regulate male and female organs during puberty, regulate metabolism)

12. The systems of the human body are independent and function on their own. (F)

13. There are different three types of muscles. (T)

14. Reproduction ensures the survival of humans as a species. (T)

15. The endocrine system is a network of glands located throughout the body that are all the same shapes and sizes. (F)

16. The human body is complex and multi-cellular organism. (T)

17. The liver, kidneys and brain all act like a filter to remove waste from the body. (F)

18. Excess fluids called urine are stored in the bladder and excreted (when it's time to use the toilet). (T)

19. The digestive system processes the nutrients from the food that can be by the cells to make energy, so food is really fuel.(T)

20. The "master glands" that controls all the other glands is called the pancreas. (F)

# Chapter 7:

1. The process of a male and female bird finding a mate so they can reproduce is called **courtship**.

2. Some animals like amphibians and insects go through a complete change from egg to adult called a **metamorphosis**.

3. The stages in the life cycle of many insects such as the bee are **egg, larva, pupa** and **adult.**

4. An **adult** is the term for a full-grown, mature animal or plant.

5. A seed is **dormant**, which means it is resting, waiting for the right conditions to sprout.

6. **Fertilization** occurs when a female and male of a species get together and mix the sperm and an egg.

7. A developing baby inside a mother's uterus is called a **fetus.**


8. **Bee**: egg, larva, pupa, adult

9. **Human:** egg, baby, childhood, adolescent, adult

10. **Frog:** egg, tadpole, adult

11. **Bird:** egg, chick, nestling, fledglings, adult


12. Adolescents are mature and fully-grown. (F)

13. Germination is the birth of a plant. (T)

14. Only animal organisms have life cycles. (F)

15. Pollination is the process of pollen being transferred from the anther of to the stigma.___

(T)

16. Only the queen bee lays eggs. (T)

17. A seed is not a living thing. (F)

18. Plants have male and female flowers. (T)

19. A fledgling is a young bird that is ready to fly away and leave the nest. (T)

20. Birds go through a metamorphosis. (F)

# Chapter 8:

1. The noise cause by a sonic wave because of lightning is called **thunder**.

2. Long periods of light rain or drizzle is often caused by a **warm front**.

3. Winds caused temperature variations between the equator and the poles and the spin of the Earth cause the **Coriolis Effect**.

4. **Climate** is the temperature and type of weather of a region or area over the course of years.

5. The unequal heating of the Earth's **atmosphere** is the main cause of weather.

6. A **cold front** produces heavy rains, gusty winds and possible thunderstorms.

7. Clouds that form at the surface of the Earth are called **fog.**

8. During a thunderstorm is it safest to be **indoors**.

9. Thunderstorms are cause by cumulonimbus clouds and produce gusty winds, **heavy rains**, and sometimes thunder, lightning and hail.

10. The rotation or cycle of cool air and warm air causes **wind.**

11. **Condensation** is the part of the water cycle in which clouds are formed.

12. **Cirrus** clouds are the highest clouds, are very cold, and are usually made of ice crystals.

13. Tornadoes can sometime occur when at cold front catches up to a warm front, which is called an **occluded front**.

14. Rain, snow, sleet and hail are all types of **precipitation**.

15. Warm air is lighter than cool air, and so warm air **rises**.

16. The low, flat, grey clouds that cover the entire sky and cause drizzle are called **stratus**.

17. The sun heats the atmosphere **unequally** and this causes differences in temperature and pressure that creates weather.

18. What is the difference between weather and climate? *Weather is the result of pressure and temperature and can change from day-to-day and season-to-season. Climate is the average temperature and weather of a place over a long period of time.*

19. What are weather fronts and what do they cause? *A cold front is when advancing cold air meets warm air. They bring heavy rain, gusty winds and thunderstorms. A warm front is when advancing warm air meets cold air. They bring long periods of drizzle.*

20. What are the differences between cloud types? *Cumulus clouds are big, puffy, white clouds. If there are changes in pressure and temperature, they can become cumulonimbus clouds. These are tall towering cumulus clouds also known as thunderstorm clouds. Cirrus clouds are high, wispy thin clouds and are the highest clouds of all. Cirrus clouds are usually made of ice crystals. They are a good indicator that more pleasant weather is on the way. Stratus are the low, flat, grey clouds that cover the entire sky and cause drizzle. Fog is a low laying cloud that forms at the surface of the Earth.*

# Chapter 9:

1. The crust of the Earth is composed of three types of rocks: igneous, metamorphic and **sedimentary**.

2. The movement of sediment by water, wind or gravity is called **erosion**.

3. The Earth's layers are the crust, **mantle**, outer core and inner core.

4. An example of deposition at the mouth of a river is called a **delta**.

5. The Earth is composed primarily of **rock**.

6. The **rock cycle** is a process of the Earth changing rocks from igneous to metamorphic to sedimentary and back to igneous.


7. **Weathering**          Process that rock is worn away and broke down

                by wind and rain


8. **Igneous**          A type of rock formed when magma cools and

                    hardens


9. **Glacier**          Massive, slow moving amounts of ice that can

                    carve valleys and deposit sediment


10. **Deposition**          The depositing of sediments due to erosion

11. **Continents**          The landmasses on the Earth's surface

11. **Soil**          Dirt or earth

12. Continental drift is the movement of plates of the crust on top of the mantle. (T)

13. Fossils can be found most often in sedimentary rock. (T)

14. Scientists that study the earth and how it changes are called biologists. (F)

15. When two plates move sideways against each other they eventually slip. If pressure is released suddenly, the plates will jerk apart causing a volcano.  (F)

16. Because humans cannot travel or drill below the surface to great depths below the surface of the Earth, geologist must hypothesis about the composition of the inner and outer core. (T)

17. Soil is made of minerals, water, air, organic material (dead plants and animals), but not bacteria. (F)

18. Metamorphic rock is formed deep in the Earth's crust where heat and pressure causes rock to undergo a metamorphosis. (T)

19. How is the Earth like a hardboiled egg? *The crust is like the shell of an egg. The mantle is like the egg whites. The inner and outer core are like the yolk.*

20. Why is soil important to the Earth? *Soil allows for plants to grow. It gives plants a place to grow and provides plants nutrients needed to grow. It provides a habitat for animals. It also acts like a filter to clean the water on Earth.*

Made in the USA
Lexington, KY
08 December 2014